# Successful study for degrees

## Second edition

## Rob Barnes

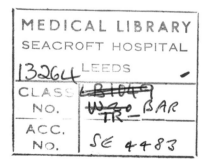

ROUTLEDGE

London and New York

First published 1992
by Routledge

Second edition published 1995
by Routledge
11 New Fetter Lane, London EC4P 4EE

Simultaneously published in the USA and Canada
by Routledge
29 West 35th Street, New York, NY 10001

Reprinted 1996

Typeset by LaserScript, Mitcham, Surrey
Printed and bound in Great Britain by
Mackays of Chatham PLC, Chatham, Kent

*British Library Cataloguing in Publication Data*
A catalogue record for this book is available
from the British Library

*Library of Congress Cataloguing in Publication Data*
A catalogue record for this book is available from
the Library of Congress

ISBN 0–415–12741–6

To C.

# Successful study for degrees

*Successful Study for Degrees* is a practical guide to studying more effectively at first and higher degree levels. Aimed primarily at students looking for more than just a basic study skills book, it blends practical ideas with sound principles, and is structured so that topics such as essay writing feed into chapters on dissertation preparation and writing. It uses many examples drawn from interviews conducted with students and lecturers from a range of disciplines.

At a time when many arts-based courses are changing in structure, particular attention is given to research-based study, which in many cases is replacing the traditional formal examination. At undergraduate level, the book gives practical guidance on reading, seminars and questioning techniques; at higher degree level, it discusses issues such as validity, reliability and meaning. The book also offers techniques of questioning to promote higher level thinking, including explorations of commonly-used terms such as proposition, premise, assumption and evidence.

**Rob Barnes** is Senior Lecturer in Education at the University of East Anglia, and has taught study skills to undergraduates and postgraduates since the early 1970s. He has published two books on art and design for primary school teachers. These, and other publications, including computer software, focus on creative thinking applied to learning. He is also a practising artist whose limited edition etchings sell internationally.

The very reason for studying is that it reveals a vision of the world you have not previously encountered.

# Contents

# Acknowledgements

I would like to thank a number of people who have influenced the writing of this book. Many students have stimulated the ideas contained here as have a number of colleagues in informal conversations.

In particular I would like to thank Cathy Whalen, Susan Halliwell, Bev Labbett and Deborah Berrill for reading and responding to some of the earlier drafts of the text. Of the many people who were interviewed, I would like to thank in particular Alan Simpson and Professors Richard Sheppard and Charles Desforges.

RB

# Chapter 1

# What makes a good learner?

> It's all lies, really. I put on my application form that I wanted the discipline of a long course. One that would stimulate, excite and give me contact with intellectuals. Now I'm here, I have difficulty getting started . . . everyone else seems much more intelligent and hard-working than I am.
>
> (Student)

The shortest answer I can find to the question 'What makes a good learner?' is 'One who can get started'. There is some truth in this over-simplification, verified by experience of leaving essays, revision and dissertations to the last minute. Plausible reasons to do something else instead flood into the mind. So does the picture of study for a degree being solitary confinement with books, notes and, if you are lucky, a word-processor. The mental image is completed if the study is done alone, surrounded by stale coffee mugs, yesterday's cooking, in an unheated room, in the middle of winter, while wearing three layers of clothing.

If 'getting started' is daunting, preparing to start is much more attractive. As an antidote to the loneliness of studying for a degree, you may well find all manner of activities can be undertaken to avoid actually starting. First go to the library and take out as many books as you can. Next buy yet another pen, pencil, A4 notepad and yet more card index refills. Now you are ready to start. Except, that is, for a cup of coffee, a quick snack, a look at today's paper and the television news. Now you are ready to start. Except that you remember that a vital piece of information for your study is being dealt with in tomorrow's seminar. Frankly, it would be much better to wait until then. In any case, look at the clock.

## MYSTIQUE, MYTHS AND HANGUPS

For many students, academic study at degree level is shrouded in mystery. Particularly at first degree level, time can be wasted in trying to fathom what lecturers want from you in order to award the degree. Such guesswork is wasted energy because, in truth, two students can be awarded the same degree for quite different content, style and contribution. Provided their work is of degree standard, there can be wide variation in each student's response. Your degree may require you to spend most of your time in the library. Another student will need to spend time gathering research data and analysing it. Research methods vary and you may need to choose between 'statistical', 'hypothetico-deductive', 'ethnographic', 'descriptive' or 'action-research' modes. Attempting to discover what constitutes degree standard is therefore inappropriate because you have no experience of the quality which your degree will demand.

A far better strategy is to discover what skills, attitudes and experience lecturers are trying to encourage. Do they want you to debate issues? Do they want you to test your assumptions and wrestle with conflicting opinions? What do they hope you can do by the end of the year? How do they think you might go about it?

If there is a mystique, this may be because your view of a degree is unreal. Some students see a degree as something strange out there, wrapped up in a secret code. Their approach is to search for cryptic clues to unravel the code which they think is known only to the lecturing staff. If you believe that a secret code exists, your aim, quite naturally, is to crack the code and 'get' the degree. The reality is that you will be awarded a degree if the quality of your work merits it.

> When I first started this degree course, I never imagined you could go on and on finding deeper and deeper levels of meaning. I imagined there was a limited amount of knowledge necessary for this degree. But now I have to put my own parameters on it and decide when to stop. You just can't study everything, so you have to make choices. Study for me is about making the best choices I can.
>
> (Law student)

This student is not trying to crack any codes. If you think there is something hidden or subversive about a degree, then your study is rather like a shifty car sale. You are led to believe that only a certain amount of dishonest trading will save the day and the only way to gain a degree is to 'beat the system'. Naturally, there are times when you may think your degree course is obscured by jargon and lecturers may seem confusing in their aims. Yet it is just as likely that your attention has focused on an abstract notion of 'the degree', rather than on your contribution to it. All degree subjects develop specialized language and some use technical jargon as a way of dealing with details. Jargon is only an additional irritation for students starting a degree course, not the main reason why they feel there is a mystique. Beating the system may seem like a challenge, but it is not the best way to benefit from your degree.

The myth of a university being an 'ivory tower' is unfortunately still widespread. To an outsider, academics can seem like self indulgent superbrains. Impractical, absent-minded, arrogant and elitist are all adjectives which have been used to describe them in the past. These excesses are wildly inaccurate for the majority of academics teaching on your degree course, even if the myth is traditional. Studying for a degree is not something which is understood only by arrogant members of an academic elite. There is no academic 'club' for you to join and no intention to keep you in the dark. Many academics would be the first to admit to under-confidence about their own study and research. Even so, your impression of them can be a distorted one, especially if they have just written a critical report on your essay. Their manner can be misread. As one lecturer remembers:

> When I first went to university I remember being reduced to a gibbering idiot every time I spoke to my teacher. He was distinguished both in his grey-haired appearance and in his academic achievements. It wasn't his fault, but he sounded so much like a news bulletin that I felt a fool whenever I tried to string a sentence together. Gradually things got better and I realized he wasn't really criticizing my every word, but this was just his personal style. During my course I got to know him quite well and one evening we talked about how sounding intelligent could actually be quite threatening. He put his head in his hands and said 'I really wish I didn't have that effect on people, you know. I wish in a way I hadn't developed such a fluency with words. It's dogged me ever since.'

If fluency with words is intimidating, then the sight of other students exuding an air of apparent self-assurance does nothing for your own confidence. You may even feel guilty at the sight of so many students with their noses into books when yours is not. Many of them seem poised and in control of their destinies. Nobody is ready to take you aside and explain how to go about starting your study because they know nothing of your own learning style. Where are the short-cuts? If you are a mature student, it may be years since you last wrote an essay. If you are straight from school you may be devastated to discover your motivation to study by yourself is abysmal when compared with the pressure to work if teachers pushed you on. Here, the only deadline you may have during the academic term is a distant long assignment due in after the vacation. Your study is in your own hands, but you are not sure where to begin.

Brilliant students exist, but the 'super-student' (mentioned in numerous books about study) is just another myth. We can dispense with this figment of the imagination at the outset. 'Super-student' is probably created by you as a result of reading the fine print of your degree too carefully. Setting yourself against an idealized image of the perfect student is almost bound to result in a poor attitude to study. The traditional myth is that 'super-students' read all the books on the reading list, are always organized, take perfect notes in lectures, study in preference to meeting friends, have excellent memories and are super-confident. They are never lost in seminars, never suffer from anxiety and self-doubt, find writing essays easy and love every minute of their final examinations. They are always on time for lectures, ask relevant and searching questions, are well liked, have a sense of humour, manage their finances to perfection and gain the highest possible grades. In their spare time they service the car, win prizes for making their own wine, play the French horn, violin, guitar and serpent. When they are not doing this, they edit the student newsletter, produce gourmet dinners, go hang-gliding, motor-racing and climb Mont Blanc.

Nothing is more likely to make students feel ignorant than the deception that others are more vocal, much brighter and considerably better than they are. My experience has been that students who have plenty to say in seminars do not necessarily make the best contribution or turn in the best essays. I sometimes wish I could hear all the intelligent thoughts which stay in students' heads during seminars. I know of many students who, when pressed, have an excellent contribution to make, but would not dream of offering it in a group unless they were prompted. Many admit to the fear of looking foolish. They have self-doubts, which is a healthy sign that they are questioning their own values and do not suffer from the ignorance of absolute certainty. If you never had the slightest doubt about anything, how would you ever raise questions and discuss issues? Seeking ways to be a 'super-student' is a handicap you cannot afford to indulge. Settle for being human instead.

## SUCCESSFUL STUDY

There are a number of practical steps you can take to study more effectively. It is tempting to think that there is a large element of luck attached to success and failure, but at degree level luck can be only a very small factor. Failing your degree can happen in two particular ways. The first of these results from misjudging require-ments and the second from not really wanting to study at all. This book is about helping you to avoid the first kind of failure by making better judgements regarding why, what and how you study. It gives examples of writing techniques and suggests structures for dissertations and assignments. The topics discussed are based on interviews with a wide spectrum of students and lecturers. If you do not want to study at all there is no known cure for that. But you might need to clarify your mind on this second reason to fail, because motivation to study is vital if you are to understand your own situation.

Why do people study for a degree? Is it for the sheer enjoyment of stretching the mind? Is it the attraction of varied study likely to be found in a combined degree? Is it to reap the rewards of the degree course itself? Is it to become more employable with a higher qualification? Is it to impress other people that you can gain a degree? Is it that it seemed the natural 'next step' and there was nothing better to do? All of these are acceptable reasons to study and some of them will motivate you more than others. Your own study habits and your success are most likely to be governed by how well you know yourself and how genuinely serious you are about studying. As Phillips and Pugh (1987: 30) point out, some students think it would be rather nice to have a PhD, in the same way that it would be nice to be a millionaire. This is not the same as knowing you really want a degree and why you want it. If you really do want a degree, there will be times when you choose a study routine rather than lead a full social life. You know what you want so you strike a bargain with yourself. Something like, 'Study now and endure the pain because universities do not award degrees for doing nothing', or 'Go out with friends another night because this essay can't wait any longer.' In other words, the payoff you perceive becomes more motivating than any distractions. Successful study depends on knowing your own situation and knowing what you really want.

Of course, the reward of a degree can seem a long way off. In the short term, it is much more difficult to sustain motivation for study. A further deception, however, is that students who study all the time are automatically more successful than those who have a social life. There is no evidence to suggest that they are. I believe that successful students give themselves short-term rewards and do not necessarily have to choose between work and leisure. If you are going to choose between study and doing something else, then the payoff has to be made worthwhile. But as we see here, your success can depend on the bargain you make with yourself:

> What motivates me to choose between a social life and study? The answer is I don't choose between them. I don't stay in and miss the social life because the social life is my reward for studying. I organize my life so that I study for a certain time before the night life. Sometimes I will study one night in order to go out another. Mostly I study during the day or early evening knowing I have a reward lined up for later.
>
> (Law student)

There are rewards more closely associated with studying itself. Not all the study you do is a chore and many students find that writing an essay or reading a book elates them because they become aware of what they have achieved or understood. In a nutshell, they have provided their own positive feedback which is essential for them to succeed. Whereas at school you were used to producing short essays and seeing your teacher very frequently, this is not so typical of higher education. Written assignments, for example, tend to be much longer in length, but fewer in number. Feedback, in terms of marks, grades and comments, generally takes longer to filter back to you than it would at school. You may spend a considerable time wondering what the degree is all about, and the longer the feedback on your progress takes, the less you may actually want to hear about it.

Short-term rewards depend on the feedback you are able to devise for yourself when you study. For example, studying ten pages of a book for an hour can be rewarding provided your feedback system tells you what you gained from it. You might choose to make a mental map of the structure, look for links between sections, try to memorize the sequence of points made, look for the main issues or be aware of controversy. Here is the reward. You would have reduced the study to a smaller self-imposed task and looked for something *specific* rather than studied in a random fashion. Once you had noted the main points or drawn your own 'route-map' of the content you could compare it with the original chapter. The self-assessment you devised would help you to monitor your progress. A sense of achievement would come through being in control of your study and knowing what you were trying to do, even if you did not do it to perfection. Significantly, you would have put your own parameters on the task.

Successful students, I would argue, are those who are in charge of their own learning. Your style of learning is not the same as mine or anyone else's, which is why only you can be in control of it. Students who find it difficult to 'get started' have not genuinely taken charge of their learning and found ways to organize it. Their social life is not seen as a reward for study, but as an anaesthetic to the study which is still waiting to be tackled. Maybe before examinations social life takes a temporary back seat, but successful study does not mean you are a hermit. The deal is a simple one. If you want to be in control and have a social life, the price to pay is to develop a few organized study habits, preferably those which give you the best feedback.

The strategy which I believe works best, is to keep your organization to the absolute minimum designed to keep you in control of your study. Not everyone likes an organized life, but in studying for a degree there has to be at least some time devoted to organization. The example of reading ten pages is a useful one to pursue. Clearly, if you decide to study ten pages with a specific aim in mind, you need a rough idea of when to tackle the next ten pages. The very fact that you decided to study ten pages shows you have preferences and can make a decision. But does the remainder of the material you want to study stay in the back of your mind as a mixed bag of tasks? What will you next take out of the bag? You may need to sketch out a rough plan of events, even if you know that your rough plan will change. Like the law student who spoke of deeper and deeper meanings, you must choose how you plan your study because there will always be too much to study. Otherwise, your study will drift towards panic at the last minute.

## HOW TO GET THE BEST FROM THIS BOOK

Numerous research studies of study methods have been undertaken in the past. Books and papers provide evidence of study problems, not all of which reach the person who matters most – you, the student. Two particular projects (Entwistle and Wilson 1977; Marton *et al.* 1984) reveal excellent pictures of student study for academic awards. Reference is made to these throughout the book and you may find the Marton research particularly useful if you are looking for evidence about study strategies.

The structure of this book allows you to dip into chapters such as those on examination techniques and writing dissertations. There are one or two study strategies which are 'dead ends' and knowing about them can save you frustration. Chapter 2 deals with just such a theme. Chapter 3 suggests a number of short-cuts to organizing your study and Chapter 4 deals with essential questions at a much higher level of study than previous chapters. The material on essay writing feeds directly into the chapters about dissertations. After reading the first four chapters, you will discover that your own needs will determine which material is relevant to you.

Research styles present students with very different problems and chapters include references to action-research besides more traditional approaches. Essays and dissertations call for similar skills even if their style differs according to the activity undertaken. You will need to ensure that the information you extract from chapters applies to you.

Each chapter ends with a check list summary and an action plan. These cover the main issues which are raised, but you cannot derive the best from this book unless you actually try out some of the suggestions for yourself. Reading them, without turning them over in your mind, is a passive way to study. Studying them is an active way to read.

**CHECK LIST SUMMARY**

- You will succeed if your view of a degree is realistic.
- Successful study depends on devising feedback which helps you.
- To be in control of your study, you must make choices and organize your study habits.
- Being in control of your study means you must know the requirements of your degree.

**ACTION PLAN**

- Write down what areas of study you think you need most help to improve.
- Look at the contents of this book and write down the areas of study that interest you most.
- Write down any ways you can think of to devise feedback for your study.
- Try to find out some of the skills and understanding you might expect to develop on your course.
- Make some attempt to discover what you really want from your degree.

# Chapter 2

# Having, being and study

In a powerfully influential book, Eric Fromm (1979) argued that a fundamental block to effective study was the notion that students could 'have' knowledge. You may well think this way yourself as books, notes, essays and assignments become possessions that mean a great deal to you. Handing over a dissertation for marking can sometimes feel like giving away your own child, so strong is the attachment. Yet knowledge or learning, whatever you take them to be, are unlikely to be 'things' that we 'have'. Fromm saw them more as signs of our understanding at a particular moment. His ideas went much further than discussing study and his book *To Have or To Be?* is still relevant today. I have drawn freely on some of his ideas and related them to study.

## TWO WAYS OF LEARNING

The 'having' mode of study is evident whenever we see study as something permanent to 'have'. All we need to discover, is how to 'have' and own it. Our view of degree study is that whoever designed the course has set aside a fixed amount of knowledge and once we have this knowledge we are awarded a qualification. Students, argues Fromm, in the having mode of existence, will listen to a lecture in order to copy down notes as best they can to memorize later on. They transform what they hear into fixed clusters of thought or theories that they store up. The content of the lecture does not become part of them in any enriching way. Student and lecture are strangers to each other because the student has become the owner of a collection of statements made by somebody else.

Most lectures and books contain material that occurs between important statements, and this is vital to the way in which we process ideas. In the having mode of study, we are likely to ignore any lecture material that exists between statements as if it were redundant. An obstacle to effective study exists if students see only other people's statements and ideas as worth their attention. Their concern is to try to make their version of what they assume to be the lecturer's notes. They ignore the part of a lecture that might be the most active because it cannot easily be copied down. Similarly, they look for statements in books and underline them in pencil to make them theirs. This is quite different from underlining ideas or questions (see Chapters 4 and 7). The problem is one of 'statement collection' versus 'ideas collection'.

To a certain extent, we all want to hold on to knowledge as statements and information. The trouble with this is that new ideas can be particularly threatening. If we see our lecture notes as fixed statements or information to be memorized, the last thing we want to happen is that someone comes along to change them. A further difficulty in the having mode is that ideas which cannot easily be written down as statements can be rather frightening because they are out of our control. The sheer size of the problem frustrates the need to capture them on paper.

For example, the ideas of a writer such as Hofstadter (1985) concern the sophisticated relationship between Mathematics, Music and Art. Yet his ideas are difficult to summarize in note form because they depend on the writer's use of example after example and analogy after analogy, building towards a much greater vision. He is almost impossible to quote without including several paragraphs of text. In isolation, each statement he makes is meaningless; each analogy ridiculous without its context. The ideas depend on each other for their meaning. To 'have' Hofstadter's statements is to ignore his ideas.

The 'being' mode of existence is when, according to Fromm, we are already occupied and involved with the topic of the lecture. In the being mode, what we hear stimulates our own thought processes, giving rise to new ideas and change. We are active participants in learning because we are trying to understand concepts and issues, rather than to possess knowledge.

*Having* knowledge is taking and keeping possession of available knowledge (information); *knowing* is functional and part of the process of productive thinking.

(Fromm 1979: 47)

In other words, if we are only collecting information, it is unlikely that our thought processes are working to build a better understanding of the material to hand. We are not asking ourselves questions. The focus of our attention does not leave much room for anything else, except collecting other people's thoughts. In the being mode, our concern is rather different from this. We are trying to penetrate statements and information to raise issues, analyse and test assumptions for ourselves. We are trying to dwell in ideas and understand them.

So far, I have painted a picture that might well suggest that good students do not copy down statements and underline passages in books. Nothing could be further from the truth. In the being mode, students are extremely active in taking notes or extracting statements as part of their study. The difference is that they are not dealing with statements alone and treating them passively or regarding them as fixed knowledge. They gather nothing without trying to process it. In lectures, they do not try to record only the statements and ignore the apparent 'waffle'. When they listen, they are not checking statements against their own opinion merely to see if the statements fit what they already believe. They are actively thinking about the issues raised by statements as they follow them. By transforming information to understand it, rather than transforming it into fixed clusters of thought, their brains are not left in neutral gear.

The having mode is like a disease in which the main symptom is to be concerned with the quantity of notes and information rather than with their quality. This, I would argue, is because success is perceived as doing more study, collecting more knowledge and working the longest possible hours. If students do not do well, they assume that they need to do more in respect of quantity or time. Students who receive low marks in their essay will sometimes ask 'What more could I have done?' On closer examination of the question, it frequently turns out that they feel victims of an injustice. They worked well beyond midnight. They gave the essay everything they possibly could regarding time, words and information.

## BEING AND REMEMBERING

An obvious reason for writing down notes is to remember them. Naturally, many students will say they worry that they will not remember the content of lectures in order to pass examinations. Some degrees, such as law, demand that students remember facts and vast amounts of information. Yet there is a considerable difference between remembering to regurgitate information and remembering as a way to trigger discussion of relevant ideas or issues. In the having mode, there is a strong element of repetitive learning. The information learned this way is useful, but not necessarily memorable. A student trying to remember it frequently fails to do so because it lacks meaning.

A characteristic of forgetting anything is that it makes a weak impression (Russell 1979: 81–170). In the having mode, we are likely to rely on the brain's ability to remember information in a passive, rather detached way and strong impressions are difficult to generate. Unless we are sure that we will need the information in day to day living, or for an examination, the motivation to remember is minimal. Without a strong impression, it becomes very difficult to reconstruct the original information or event. Memory, after all, is about reconstruction of previous information or experience. Although we may say we 'have a good memory', Fromm would argue that memory is not something anyone can have because there is nothing to have. Remembering is something we do, by recalling images and events that previously made an impression. Having a good memory refers to the faculty to remember and not the recollected impression itself. As Fromm argues, we are so accustomed to using the having mode in our language that we can be convinced that intangible functions like memory can be possessed. Recalling is a function of the being mode: an active process rather than a fixed accumulated body of information.

What are the implications for study in the being mode? Clearly, if you cannot recall information when you need it for examinations, you will not succeed. But what happens if examination questions are about understanding ideas rather than supplying information? What happens if you cannot remember the issues? What happens if your head is packed with information, but you have no idea what to do with it?

When students memorize in the being mode, they try to make their material impressionable. They concentrate on a summary outline of the material and try to bring it to life in their mind by looking for meaning. If you doubt the value of this, try to test it for yourself. Compare gathering information with trying to remember the sequence of a lecture and its main issues. Ask yourself the following:

- How does one part of the information relate to another?
- What are the main issues or topics of controversy raised by the information contained in the lecture?
- What questions are worth copying down?
- Is the structure like one main planet with several satellites encircling it?
- Is the structure like a pile of similar-sized bricks constructing a great wall?

A good summary of a lecture sequence, or its structure, is often far more useful than extensive notes as a means of stimulating memory (Buzan 1974: 68–95). Why? Because it is an active reminder, a mental map that prompts the brain to reconstruct with meaning. We are far more likely to remember something that we understand than we are to remember a collection of statements which appear to be recording the content of a lecture. As several writers will testify (e.g. Russell 1979; Norman 1982; Rowntree 1988), if we have not attached meaning by processing information at a much deeper level, it is almost impossible to recall it.

## HAVING AN OPINION

The having and being modes of study are also true of conversation and seminars. You and I might have different opinions about the same subject. Imagine you view football as a major force for good, while I regard it as solely fit for hooligans. Each of us identifies with our own opinion, to the extent that (from Fromm's viewpoint) what matters to each is to find more reasonable arguments to defend our position. If you are flexible, we might just have a discussion, but if we are both in *possession* of our opinions, we are afraid of losing them. The result is a battle of words to support a narrow point of view and save our own skin. I might concentrate exclusively on the bad behaviour of supporters, while you will possibly emphasize the power of team spirit, excitement and physical well-being to be experienced. A personal opinion is just that. Unless it can be informed by agreed data, there is little chance of our ever having a discussion. To win the argument, I must leave out certain aspects, ignore my own contradictions and evade the issues that you raise. If you win the argument, then I will probably feel insecure. My feelings of security depend on reassuring myself that my fixed opinion is 'right'.

If we are conversing in the being mode, things are rather different. You are already familiar with chewing over ideas and opinions without feeling threatened. You have less difficulty discussing your ideas because they can be modified spontaneously as the discussion progresses. Furthermore, you are ready to explain and express your ideas because you do not bury them in the back of a storehouse as fixed opinions or statements. You share opinions rather than use them as ammunition. Changing your opinion is not threatening because you are not attached to your views.

## EXAMINATIONS

A sense of security in the having mode can only be achieved by having enough information stored to make us feel safe. Consequently, we can feel insecure if our own need to collect and memorize is so unrealistic that it can never be satisfied. Collecting and memorizing can go on forever. In the being mode, we have already tried to think what all the information was about and are well ahead when it comes to making our mark in examinations. The having mode leads to a fear of being tested on the information we hope to have memorized. In the having mode, not to study fuels the fear of being tested.

I was trying to guess what sort of information they might ask me in the exam. [having mode]

I was trying to understand the issues that might come up in the exam. [being mode]

At university I was known as 'rent a hand' because I would take down notes verbatim. I had this obsession with getting it all down. At exam time I'd be up at 6 o'clock in the morning trying to memorize things.

(Geography graduate)

In lectures I'd be in the being mode, using ideas as a springboard to go off and read for discussion in seminars . . . but when it came to exams, I was in the having mode, trying to cram information for a three-hour exam to get my degree.

(Sociology graduate)

Examinations, more than any other academic activity, are likely to panic students into the having mode. If this happens to you it is not necessarily a disaster because extremely intensive reading can sometimes lead to better understanding. Even so, in the being mode, students are much more likely to study for their own development and understanding. The examination answers they give will be quite different from those which stop short of deeper meaning. To study in the being mode gives them insight and develops the expression of their ability, talents and interests.

## EVERYDAY LANGUAGE AND LEARNING

To understand how deeply ingrained the having mode can become, we must look much further than study. Fromm argues that the having mode appears to be more natural in a society used to acquiring property and making a profit. The being mode is difficult to perceive and understand once we have set the dominant pattern of having. Within a pattern of having, it is much more difficult to be an outsider and not conform to that which we see as the cultural norm. In a society where we take having for granted as the way of existing, being is illogical, unconventional and fits uncomfortably within a culture used to material wealth.

As evidence, Fromm gives examples from everyday language of the way we express ourselves in the having mode. We say we have an illness, rather than are ill, and have a problem rather than find things difficult. More recent than Fromm's examples are phrases like, 'I'm having a hard time right now', rather than 'this is very hard to do'. We refer to my doctor, my dentist and my bank as if we own them. Having refers to things that we can describe as objects or 'things' to have. Fromm's being mode of existence refers to experience which, he argues, is in principle indescribable.

## STUDYING IN THE BEING MODE

I have described the having mode rather like a list of unpleasant ailments. Fromm constructs these two polarities to make his point more forcibly and, in practice, you will study in both the having and being modes. Your active lecture notes and reminders of the meanings you extracted are likely to become important possessions. They are important because of what they will trigger in an active mind. Mental maps, reminders, essays and assignments made in the being mode of study are precisely what you might need to hang on to so that you can function. Notes, scribbled on the back of an envelope, become essential ingredients for success in understanding your study. At least, you could feel pretty bad about losing them if they generated streams of thought and summarized the main issues of a lecture or a book. They are valuable for what they are likely to do for you when that crucial examination or dissertation looms. There might be all the more reason to have them safely in your possession.

The conflict between a desire to understand and the need to possess can be resolved by thinking of the being mode as 'active' learning. Fromm's main contention is that there is 'passive' and 'active' learning. The having mode is deadly dull and passive when compared with studying actively in the being mode. It is passive because information and ideas leave only a faint trace within the brain. Very little happens except hearing, seeing, reading or recording in order to capture and possess. If students are 'active', they learn by doing something with their study. Paragraphs that they write are more likely to analyse, criticize, develop or link ideas to make a point. In lectures, students in the being mode are far more concerned to come out of the room turning over an issue in their mind, than they are to feel reassured about 'getting it all written down'.

You will still need to take notes and revise from them. The most passive learning is where a student takes no notes and does nothing with the ideas or statements on offer. That state of affairs could lead to the award of a degree simply for sitting politely during lectures. On the other hand, no amount of writing, searching a library or reading from cover to cover indicates 'active' learning. The absence of intense, busy, physical activity is also not an indicator of passive learning. Being active, in Fromm's analysis, is an inner experience, it is not just the busyness of outer activity: the good student already thinks about what to do with study material rather than locks it away.

One means of approaching learning might be deliberately to reject passive forms of study wherever you suspect you indulge in them. If you can recognize the signs that learning has become something in which you are not particularly active (mentally), you might just as well reject it anyway. Of course, you will no doubt feel you must fill the vacuum with something else, but Fromm would argue that abandoning the desire to possess knowledge in the having mode is a good beginning. In studying, passivity excludes activity; activity excludes passivity.

The clearest description of the active being mode is, in my view, provided through a symbol suggested to Fromm by Max Hunziger.

> A blue glass appears to be blue when light shines through it because it absorbs all colours and thus does not let them pass. That is to say, we call a glass 'blue' precisely because it does not retain the blue waves. It is named not for what it possesses, but for what it gives out.
>
> (Fromm 1979: 92)

Making good use of your study time will involve all the traditional activities like taking notes, writing essays and collecting information. What counts as 'blue light' is what we actively give out after processing the material before us. This, I would argue, is exactly what well-constructed examinations and assignments assess. No processing, no blue light.

A nightmare vision of study is one where learning is finite, confined to an immutable collection of lectures and books, thoughts and statements, fixed for all time. Fortunately, many lectures already involve active learning by including 'workshop' tasks which the lecturer sets. The formal lecture, as a means of teaching, is often criticized for being far too passive and many lecturers recognize this drawback. Sometimes the purpose of these 'workshop'-cum-lecture sessions is to keep students involved and active. The lecturer will typically take a break from lecturing and spend twenty minutes or so working with small groups of students. You will be set a problem to discuss or possibly given a task, written down on a sheet of paper. Often this contains information which needs to be learned or memorized. What matters, however, is what you do with the information that you encounter.

## CHECK LIST SUMMARY

| | |
|---|---|
| Having | Being |
| Passive | Active |
| Fixed ideas | Ideas change |
| Dependent on possession | Independent of possession |
| Insecurity generated | Confidence generated |
| Isolated ideas and unrelated statements | Ideas are linked and statements compared |
| Links not important | Links important |
| Brain in neutral | Brain is processing |
| Excludes activity | Excludes passivity |
| Fear of losing argument | Intrigued by different views |
| Fear of being tested | Enhanced understanding |
| Concern for facts and information | Concern for meaning and issues |
| Collecting | Questioning |
| No comparisons | Compare/contrast |
| Accept only what you agree with | Consider areas of conflict |
| Threatened by new ideas | New ideas sustain interest |
| Narrow view of topics | Wide view of topics |
| Do nothing with information | Transform information |

## ACTION PLAN

- Decide whether or not to do anything with what follows.
- Write down examples of passive study you can remember from your own experience.
- Write down any questions this chapter raises for you.
- Ask yourself how accurate for you personally are the equations: to have = passive; to be = active.

# Chapter 3

# Short-cuts: a summary of study skills

Suppose you wanted to read a book from cover to cover in the shortest possible time. You would lock yourself away in a room and not emerge until the last page was read. In theory this would be an efficient way to read, but in practice your study habits need to be designed to cope with interruptions and a million and one demands on your time. Some books and essays will be so engrossing that there is no problem giving time to them. Others will seem like an imposition and you will not easily believe in what you are doing.

Most students at some point suffer from overkill. Too many demands are made all at the same time, the whole system grinds to a halt, and they lose control of their study. Without a minimum of organization, they can claim to be victims of circumstance and outside forces. Charles Handy (Handy and Aitken 1986: 55) suggests that we allocate responsibility for success and failure according to the way in which we need to protect ourselves. We generally accept responsibility for success, but blame failure on external events or on other people.

> If you've got too much to do you can justify not functioning well. If you have a breakdown you can go away and think, 'It was unfair to make these demands on me, therefore external factors are to blame for it because I was doing my best.' But there's nothing creative in that. What you do is to make something a priority and pull it into the foreground. You make it your thing that you do well.
>
> (Teacher)

When study is unmanageable, the feelings students report are like having too many bills to pay. The more bills there are, the less likely it is that even one bill will be paid. The analogy of debt is a useful one. Debt counsellors recall numerous cases where people seriously in debt would not open their post any more. The role of a debt counsellor is often to break down debts into more manageable payments and so reduce the psychological pressure. The same principle can be applied to study. Unless we can limit our perception of study, and reduce the pressure, we are likely to disengage from it and stop studying altogether.

A theme, to which I will return throughout this book, is 'pulling something into the foreground'. That applies as much to study tasks as it does to time management. Ten ideas will have little impact unless one or two of them are pulled into the foreground. The same is true of finding time for ten tasks or studying ten chapters of a book. Short-cuts to study could easily come in tens or hundreds, but how many can you focus on to make sense of your own situation? In my view, there are two important short-cuts to successful study. Neither of these is particularly new or revolutionary, but when you adapt them to your own study methods you have two powerful means to improve your success. One is to perceive study as manageable pieces; the other is to develop your questioning technique so that you study in an active way.

## MANAGEABLE PIECES

Some students make endless lists of jobs they must do. I know of one who not only makes lists, but then makes lists of the lists she has made. Then she puts the long lists aside and works from the shorter list. Another has a daily diary with a full page of jobs to be done, plus those yellow sticky 'post it' notes stuck all over the page. Both students are quite happy with their methods of managing time. Happiness can be a very long list with only two or three asterisks. As one administrator puts it, 'You clear your mind by writing things down whether you do them or not.'

A great barrier to doing anything is to perceive it as a problem. Homespun philosophy says, 'It's only a problem if you think it's a problem.' I cannot pretend to make this work every time, but the basis of the maxim is that as soon as we label things as 'problems', rather than as a combination of events, we create our own psychological prison. We become trapped by the problem we have perceived for ourselves. Naturally, there are difficulties in perceiving some events as anything but a problem. Imagine clinging to a mountain ledge by your fingertips and saying to yourself, 'It's only a problem if I think it's a problem', or 'Don't worry, falling off this mountain is only one in a series of events.' The conviction seems a difficult one to sustain. Yet, if we see a 'problem' as an awkward combination of events, then we can do our best to influence the next series of events by taking action. Study 'problems' are problems if we make no attempt to devise any actions to change things. When events change, the situation is no longer a problem in the conventional sense of the word. I realize that such a view of study may not be relevant for every student, but the truth of it is remarkably robust.

## TIME MANAGEMENT

One of the most valuable experiences in higher education is that of learning to manage time, a skill which employers are likely to rate highly. Your own success in time management cannot be created by chance, but will involve decisions about how you slice the day, week or year into pieces. That means you must have a rough idea of the way your year is mapped out, otherwise clashes of commitment are more frequent than they need be:

> I'm not sure I know what a busy person is. What is too much to do? If you say you're short of time, you really mean that you mismanaged your time or you made the wrong decisions about how to use it in the first place. We all get it wrong, don't we? If you haven't time, then you decided to do other things instead . . . it's a decision you take or maybe a regret you entertain. What makes you say, 'I've done enough'? You can't study everything can you? So you choose in the end.
>
> (Lecturer in Economics)

A principle of management is to sketch in our overall plans, then temporarily conceal some of these. That way we reveal a few of the priorities and put everything else into the background. When studying, a list with asterisks, a diary or a clipboard pulls priorities forward and leaves other work in the general fog of 'things to do when I can get round to them'. It is not that we will never do the tasks on the rest of the list. The list must be prioritized to enable us to begin. (Do you really believe you are bound to do everything on your open-ended list? Such a belief can be depressing and can raise guilt feelings, unless you can find some way to limit its impact.)

Some students prefer to use a visual aid, such as a full-year planner, but these can be rather frightening because they reveal the whole study scene rather than manageable parts. You might prefer to manage time by using a desk diary or personal organizer, one which has a week across two pages so you are not tempted to overfill it. At least with a diary, the pages can be turned over to conceal past and future. In any case, your programme of study will change in such a way that you cannot plan in detail more than a few weeks ahead. Whatever system you choose, it must be realistic and not something you start with good intentions, only to abandon later. If your list is on the top of a cornflakes packet and written in pencil, what does that matter? It must work for you.

## BUNCHED DEADLINES

Bunched deadlines torpedo time management. Essay and examination deadlines are worth knowing about in the context of the whole year because they are immovable and may well come in close succession. This is especially true of some BA courses, where most of the assignments seem to be set in the spring term. The reason is often obvious. The autumn term is devoted to teaching the material for forthcoming assignments, while the summer term is probably too full of examination marking for lecturers to want to invite essay marking. If you are unfortunate enough to have three essays due in during the same week, frankly you are attempting the impossible to finish them, and you are more likely to find yourself rearranging your study slots to compensate. *Some deadlines must be brought forward by you, not by the institution.*

Besides deadlines which are set by the institution, your own study tasks will create long-term deadlines for you. For example, if you gathered data for research through interviews and questionnaires, your next task would be to analyse the data and write it up. If a report was expected, or it formed part of a dissertation, you would need to establish a deadline which said something like, 'If I don't finish collecting data by November, the report won't be finished by Easter.' Those broad deadlines are necessary, in the same way that a glance at the whole year is worthwhile. Do you know, for example, whether you have more commitments next term than you do in the current one?

The short-term view of time management is rather a different matter from deadlines and diaries. I have spoken to students whose best study time is around 6 o'clock in the morning. Others like the idea of study periods stretching into the early hours beyond midnight.

> If you're working until 10 o'clock at night and enjoying it, that's fine. If you do that occasionally, that's fine. But if you're working regularly every night until the small hours, then you're mismanaging time much more fundamentally. The more experienced you become in your study, the more you will discover which parts of your life can be in your control and which parts are not.
>
> (Lecturer in Economics)

I am told that the way to run a successful theatre is to sell plenty of tickets in advance. If people have paid for a ticket, they will usually turn up for the performance because they have set aside that time slot in their lives in which to attend. The best way to manage your study time, in my view, is to make specific hours in your week quite regular bookings, rather than snatch two full days here and there. If your style is to take a full day, well and good, but you need to be sure this is the best way to work before you commit yourself to it. As we saw from the example provided by a Law student (Chapter 1), social life can actually be a reward for studying. By all means, buy one of those pencils with an eraser at one end and mark the study periods temporarily in your diary. That way, at least you can rearrange your study time when it is interrupted. If you have no planned timetable to abandon in the first place, your time management is definitely outside your control.

## HOW LONG DO STUDENTS SPEND ON STUDY?

In the early 1970s, when study skills courses became popular, writers such as Derek Rowntree ([1970] 1988: 70) and Tony Buzan (1974: 50–5) agreed that to study efficiently, students needed to take regular breaks of at least two and possibly ten minutes every hour. This good advice is not without its problems. Breaks occur naturally at the end of reading a chapter or writing text. Longer than five minutes can make it more difficult to return to tasks and you may, in any case, be fooling yourself about the time you spend on study. How big is the mismatch between the way you *really* manage your time and your perception of it? It is well worth writing down a record of your typical week's study to see how it worked out. If you discover that you watched television, chatted on the phone, and prepared yourself assorted snacks, you are not unique. But you need to admit to yourself that this cannot be counted as study time. Self-awareness is important because your time management depends on finding out what your *efficient* study pattern is likely to be.

As long ago as the 1960s, Maddox ([1963] 1988: 37–8) described the number of hours arts and science students spent on study and when they were at their best. In a revised version of his original book, he claims that in an average 35-hour study week, students overrate their speed of work and the amount they can accomplish in a set time. He points out that, like well-known studies which have been done on industrial output, there is a loss of efficiency for study from around 2 pm in the afternoon. Although there may be a later period of renewed energy, the tradition of 'burning the midnight oil' needs to be viewed with caution. Missed deadlines and underestimation of the workload are one reason for 'burning the midnight oil', but 'midnight oil' is still rather a romantic perception of study.

Students I have asked set great store by very simple habits, such as choosing to sit in a particular chair or finding a particular place in which to study. Many of them find they must go there from force of habit, at a specific time, without being deflected. One of my colleagues remembers that she formed a good study habit of making her regular trips to the library at the same time of day. She followed in the footsteps of another student, both of whom chose to go from breakfast to the library each day before lectures began. I realize that not every student wants to rise early to do their studying, but you might be surprised to discover how many students draft their essays and read books before breakfast.

**TIME WASTED**

Architectural design is a particular case where to spend time drawing plans is essential because it is too time consuming and expensive to experiment with concrete and plate glass. In studying for a degree, you might feel that having a planning meeting with yourself is rather a waste of time, something which is subtracted from the total study time available. Preparation can be unwelcome, especially when you are itching to start what you believe is the 'real' business of study. This is to misunderstand the nature of study. If you avoid tackling a bare minimum of advance planning, the consequences can be disastrous. For example, if you intended to gather research data, or scientific evidence, the advance plans to do this would matter a great deal. You might otherwise thoroughly enjoy tape-recording interviews, or sending out questionnaires, only to discover your original planning was flawed. You brought back data which was superficial or biased. Like the architect, time invested in advance planning saves time later on. Advance planning is actually a decision-making process. No decisions means no effective management.

Business administration courses offer a number of solutions to management. Ground rules for efficiency are their stock in trade. Not everything which applies to business, however, is useful for students, but there are still some useful parallels. One ground rule is this:

A piece of paper should pass through your hands only once.

Realistically, in business administration, this means that you make a decision about what to do with it. There are three things you can do (apart from throw it away, draw on it, or make it into a paper dart). These are do it now, do it later, or store it. This means that you choose from the following options:

- Respond immediately in person or by delegating.
- Put it on a list of jobs to be done (pending tray; mark it with 'post it' stickers; or mark priorities with an asterisk).
- File it away according to a system.

You mismanage time if you make notes from the same study book over and over again. You also mismanage if you have no means of recognizing and storing the notes that you make. Far more effective is to make notes that are clearly marked with your own reference system. Set a goal of making the kind of notes which are going to be made only once (excluding your preliminary browsing). Your study method might be to store notes and papers in six or seven cardboard boxes. Mine might be to use two or three lever-arch files and a filing cabinet. The methods matter only to you, but you certainly need to avoid spending unnecessary time searching for appropriate documents.

There must be ways to create something positive which makes your study more meaningful. You will waste time if you have not found a means to gain realistic feedback about how you study. A fundamental law of studying seems to be that there will always be mismatches between your expectations and your achievements. On the one hand, you could concentrate on all the things which went wrong and everything that fell short of your expectations. There was not enough time, you failed to understand, or you were unable to structure your thoughts. On the other hand, there are always one or two things which went well. You managed half the study, you structured some of the work, or you sorted out what books were needed for your essay. 'Having enough time', 'seeing the point', and 'creating positive feedback' are made possible by putting the mismatch to one side and celebrating what little you feel you achieved.

## TASK MANAGEMENT

Just as time management depends on breaking large periods into clearly defined smaller ones, task management is similarly approached. You need limit yourself to no more than five or six aspects of a large task. Of these you will work on *one*. The aim is to find a structure for the task which will define the limits of what is possible. The structure might take the form of a list, some headings or a flow chart. Study must not be perceived as limitless, otherwise you are likely to feel that it is overwhelming and you will put your motivation at risk.

There are various ways to take an overview of your task. It would be foolish to suppose you could apply any five headings to your essay or the chapter of a book because such a structure is far too arbitrary. Yet very successful students say that when they wanted to write a PhD thesis, they looked at various PhD theses to see how they were structured. Gibbs (1977: 108–9) points out that essay plans and model structures do not suit everyone. Some students intensely dislike working to a plan, preferring to let their structure emerge. They can barely write to their own plan, never mind one suggested by anyone else. I understand this view, but do not entirely share it. Most students, in my experience, prefer a plan which they intend to modify rather than leave things to chance. You may well decide that you would prefer your plan to emerge halfway through writing an essay and that is fine, so long as your structure eventually makes sense. My view of plans is that they are useful providing you do not follow them blindly. There is nothing worse than a fixed or rigid plan, but nothing better than one you can change to suit your needs.

Consider the following categories, as if you were browsing through a thesis, or reading an academic book:

- how the topic is introduced
- reference to the available literature
- main themes of the work
- criticism and comment on these
- summary of main points and conclusion

If you were trying to write an essay, you might not want this structure at all. Even so, it would still be of some use because an arbitrary structure is better than none. To illustrate the point, look at an example which deals with only three areas:

- main sources of conflict
- similarities and differences
- topics which are 'in the foreground'

The point here is that without a structure you have no stepping stones to take you elsewhere. An arbitrary structure gives you something to react against and modify if necessary. At least you can say that it shows you what you might reject (a point pursued in more depth in Chapters 6 and 9). The aim of any structure is to gain some control of diverse ideas. As one student comments:

> When you start studying, you find all sorts of things are relevant that you never imagined were. But you have to find a ledge to hang on to . . . I find it very reassuring that I've found some headings I can use for my dissertation  . . . it actually gives me greater freedom to do what I want. It's taken a great deal off my mind, even though I still feel a bit underconfident about starting to write.
>
> (MA student)

How can this be freedom? Surely a structure constrains rather than enables freedom? How can we be free if we must stick to a predetermined plan?

The concept of freedom is not so out of place here as it might seem. In creative essay writing (and various aspects of study can be creative), most students would prefer to feel that their writing emerged as their thoughts freely generated the text. They would probably like to feel that they could pick and choose what books to read and how they wanted to read them. Students talk about 'immersing' themselves in their subject. They talk about 'letting ideas flow' as they write. Yet to create a structure gives them freedom because headings act rather like five or six 'safe-play' areas. Freedom implies choice. Random exploration of ideas is fine for a while, but needs to be ordered in some way to make study intelligible. This may mean identifying manageable targets:

> So we get to goal setting. If you're going to run a mile and you split it into quarter miles you have four goals, four achievable targets maybe, not one. We're all different, so you might decide to do half a mile and rest, then do the other half. I might want my goals in quarter miles. It depends on the task so you can't be inflexible.
>
> (Teacher)

Your mile might be a dissertation, an examination, a book to read or a seminar to prepare. Long term, your mile could be the degree. *Provided you sustain a sound overview of the whole, this lets you concentrate on a specific part.* Whatever the task involved, it will be far more efficiently dispatched if you set achievable targets because each of these gives you much needed feedback on your progress.

## KEEPING YOUR STUDY UNDER CONTROL

In my experience, the commonest study problem that students have is a weak overview of their task. That may sound a rather abstract comment, when the nitty-gritty of study is much more to do with making notes and writing yourself reminders. There are good reasons, however, to think about sketching a mental 'map' of your study. Tony Buzan frequently refers to this means of controlling study. You have probably seen students making a summary flow chart which captures the essential features of a task. This is what I will call 'the back of an envelope trick'. Other descriptions are sketch, map or 'flyer template'. Students confine their essay structure (summary of a chapter or lecture notes) to a piece of paper about the size of a standard letter envelope. The most efficient way to remind yourself of much more detail is to use a minimum number of key words or phrases which remind you of the content. Anything more than this and you might just as well refer to the whole text in the first place. In my own mind, I envisage nothing much more elaborate than headings or a 'flow chart' that I could read at a distance of five paces.

The reason why this works so well is not quite as you might expect. You summarize the task well enough to remember it, but the real gain is that you *practise* analysing in order to make summaries. Your ability to pick out the main features is improved each time you construct an overview and the spin-off is that you become much more adept at understanding the structure of your study task. Until you have some conceptual framework in your head, there are no useful hooks on which to hang ideas. Once you are used to making summaries, these trigger more and more detail as you take control. Your 'mental map' shows you how to find your way around the text.

The 'back of an envelope' trick can be used to analyse chapters of a book. Imagine using an envelope as a bookmark. On it, your summary flow chart could be a list of page references or it might summarize five aspects of a topic. Over the course of time, you would be able to refer to these bookmarks, trapped between the pages of your study books. The envelope trick works because it directs you away from an all-embracing mega-task and towards the principal features of the text. If these overviews are manageable, you are more likely to use them frequently than you are to hide them away in a folder.

A useful variant of this method is to map your lecture or essay notes by writing down key words in the margins. (You will, in any case, have done something like this before.) Imagine you are a student whose style is to take detailed notes rather than the kind summarized on an envelope. Suppose that you next want to find material relevant to the introduction of an essay, or to a topic such as 'Conflict'. Where anything in your notes coincided with your key words, you would pencil in the margin something like 'Intro' or 'Conflict'. Later, when you wanted to write the draft of your essay, or prepare for a seminar, at least you would know where to look in your notes for details that were relevant to these key topics. Essentially, you would have created an overview of categories in which to organize your notes. You might also discover useful overlap where two different categories fitted the same piece of text.

## DEVELOPING YOUR QUESTIONING TECHNIQUE

Years ago, I was totally floored by an interview question which was so wide that I had no idea where to begin. The question was 'Will you give us some idea of what you've done in the last ten years?'

and it was probably one of those questions designed to put me at my ease in the first few minutes. What I should have said was 'Yes, where shall I start?', but I muddled through in a rather *ad-hoc* way. On reflection, I could have concentrated on the following:

- What I considered the most dramatic area of change.
- How I thought I had improved something.
- How the building I worked in had been modified.
- What the effect of government policy had been.
- How my aims had changed.

There are numerous situations in which you will meet questions that are far too wide for your purposes. Recognizing these as being too wide is an important skill, because you will need to focus your response if you are to be effective. Knowing where to start is again a matter of 'pulling something into the foreground', except that this time, you search for specific detail as your first priority. You might begin with an example, compare two things, or pick out the most important feature suggested by the question. If you are really stuck, you might be able to use the structure of past, present and future. Alternatively, you might describe details in a logical sequence.

## BASIC QUESTIONING TECHNIQUE

Not all students are natural enquirers. For some, a pattern will be set in childhood and they will need to work hard to develop their questioning skills. Quite clearly, some forms of question are more useful than others. 'How?' and 'Why?' questions are useful because they tend to generate extensive answers. 'How can you tell that your study is effective?' or 'Why should you question what lecturers say?' are two examples.

The traditional journalist's six questions are 'Who?', 'When?', 'Where?', 'What?', 'Why?' and 'How?' The first three of these tend to produce closed questions which have limited answers. There are exceptions, but closed questions invite brief answers – 'right' and 'wrong', or 'yes' and 'no' responses. Examples are: 'When was the Battle of Hastings?' or 'Do you like raspberry jelly?' By comparison, 'What?', 'How?' and 'Why?' questions elicit much wider responses and are likely to form the wording of open questions. Suppose, for example, that there was a newsworthy item such as a fire in a theatre. Journalists might typically start by asking an eye-witness something like 'What was the first thing you saw?' or

'Where were you when the fire started?', thereby generating information in chronological order. Once the starting point was established, a journalist would probably need to know where the fire broke out, when it broke out, when the alarm was raised, when the fire appliances arrived, who was there, who was missing, who was hurt, who escaped, and so on. Most of this would be very straightforward fact-gathering, with no speculation or deeper searching for issues. By contrast, a journalist might use the common device of asking:

- What was the theatre like before?
- What is it like now?
- What might it be like in the future?

These questions leave the way open for wider issues to be introduced and opinions to be reported. Where there are comparisons to be made, there may be issues to discuss and judgements to make. (The term 'issue' I take to mean any topic about which there is no general agreement.) 'Why?' and 'How?' questions might address issues such as why the fire started, how it started, how dangerous it was, how quickly it spread, how people reacted, and how it could have been prevented.

When you are studying for a degree, you will be encouraged to question what you read, what you write, what you say, and what others say. This form of questioning is a distinctly different activity from asking questions to find out information. You may question a statement which has been made, especially if you made it yourself. As a student, you are expected to do this so that you can make an intelligent and well-reasoned contribution in written or spoken form. Three useful questions are offered here as a short-cut for developing your study technique. (They are discussed in greater detail in Chapters 4, 6 and 9.)

Suppose you are writing an essay on traffic congestion in city centres. You have narrowed the topic to 'Traffic congestion: vehicle use and capacity'. In the course of writing, you make a proposition such as 'Vehicles carrying the most passengers should have priority on the roads.' To question this you can ask:

- Is it true? (And where's the evidence?)
- Is it relevant? (Does it fit my essay/discussion?)
- What are the implications? (So what happens next?)

The reason for asking the first question is to verify what you write or say. Playing the part of a sceptic, you give reasons why you think this is true and reasons, examples or circumstances in which it might not be. (There are very few, if any, absolute truths, but the search for truth of statements and propositions is still a productive means of studying.) Next, you decide whether or not your statement and reasons are relevant to the topic you are discussing. In other words, you will abandon your enquiries if the effort is wasted in irrelevancy. The discussion about traffic congestion must not, for example, deal with bus drivers' uniforms, or pedestrians and shopping, unless you have a very sound argument for including them. In academic discussion, you are expected to include material which develops a well-argued point of view. Having made a statement, and having justified it by giving reasons, you next dwell on the implications of your viewpoint. (For example, what would happen if city planners adopted the principle 'The greatest acceleration determines priority on the road'? What road transport policy would need to be implemented? How might costs be met? What might be the environmental impact?)

## ASKING QUESTIONS CAN BE THE SIGN OF A LAZY STUDENT

Most of this chapter has encouraged 'being inquisitive' as a positive trait in a student. A view shared by a number of academics I have interviewed, however, is that students who do little else except ask questions are incapable of thinking for themselves. This is particularly true if their questions are always directed towards the lecturer. Lazy thinkers will ask as many questions as they can and let others do their thinking for them. They appear to be 'active', but in practice they wait for others to have ideas. Despite all the involvement they show in seminars and discussion, they are in the 'having' mode described in the previous chapter. They rarely make propositions which might be tested, rarely give informed opinions, and rarely try to argue a case. In short, they have done so little thinking for themselves that they are practically incapable of contributing.

Students who *only* ask questions are rather like sponges soaking up whatever they can. Of course, we all encounter other people's ideas and these may eventually become part of our own perspective. The difference between lazy and active students is that active students will actually mull over ideas and do their own thinking, rather than accept statements at face value. Active students try to find answers, then formulate more questions. The next chapter deals with this in the context of higher order questioning.

## CHECK LIST SUMMARY

- Pull something into the foreground.
- 'It's only a problem if you think it's a problem.'
- You clear your mind by writing things down whether you do them or not.
- Some deadlines must be brought forward by you.
- If you have no planned timetable to abandon in the first place, then your time management is definitely out of control.
- Advance planning is a decision-making process: no decisions, no effective time management.
- A piece of paper should pass through your hands only once.
- If you're going to run a mile and you split it into quarter miles, you have four goals, four achievable targets.
- Success begins when you accept the mismatch between expectation and achievement.
- An arbitrary structure is better than no structure at all.
- Provided you have a sound overview of the whole, you will be free to concentrate on a specific part.
- To change random material into an organized resource, you test a 'map' or 'flyer template' against the text:
    1 What was it like before?
    2 What is it like now?
    3 What might it be like in the future?
    4 Is it true? (And where's the evidence?)
    5 Is it relevant? (Does it fit my essay/discussion?)
    6 What are the implications? (So what happens next?)
- Asking questions can be the sign of a lazy student.

## ACTION PLAN

- Practise memorizing sequences, such as the order of news items.
- Reflect afterwards on the task you have done.

- Keep asking yourself what you would say if you had to say something. What specific point would be most appropriate? What issue grabs your attention?
- Devise a question and try to find a situation in which to ask it.
- Pick a statement and test it yourself for its truth or evidence.
- Practise questioning by discussing notes with other students.
- Think what you need to be able to do with the 'back of an envelope' technique.
- Choose any strategy suggested in this chapter and develop an alternative model for yourself.

# Chapter 4

# Higher order questions and propositions

We have been looking in the previous chapter at how questions can help you to explore an idea, maybe something you are writing or something you read. They are good starting points, but at degree level you need to go further and ask questions that raise more complex issues. The thinking demanded of you probes more complex ideas and like most higher level thinking leads to yet more questions. Higher order questions are useful to you because they generate ideas, explore concepts and feed into seminars, essays, assignments and dissertations. Once you have read this chapter you will probably need to return to it after reading other parts of the book.

**The following seven terms are used throughout this chapter**

| | |
|---|---|
| *Statement:* | can be factual, a proposition, a premise or an assertion |
| *Proposition:* | a statement offered for consideration |
| *Assertion:* | a statement (claim), but not one for consideration |
| *Valid argument:* | one which is logical, permissible and legal |
| *Premise:* | a proposition or statement from which something else can be inferred |
| *Assumption:* | something taken for granted |
| *Issue:* | any topic about which there is no general agreement |

## HOW DO HIGHER ORDER QUESTIONS HELP?

When researchers and writers try to convey their ideas, they are often building concepts. This means they have probably already asked themselves questions and the writing and research is a form of answer. Hidden questions are rather like television news coverage that edits out the journalists' interview questions. Pressure of time is such that we frequently hear replies given as statements. Somewhere, an author or journalist has asked a question. When you are reading from a book you may not be aware a question has been posed unless you are looking for one. Questions are bound to be implied and you can extract meaning from your reading by asking 'What question might the author have asked?' Even if that proves too difficult, the very fact that you are aware there might be questions can stimulate your own enquiry.

I think it's questions that give the structure of answers. I think it's questions that extend the range of possible answers. I think it's questions that open out topics. I think it's important to get students to ask the kind of questions they think a lecturer would ask them, so they in effect become their own teachers.

(Lecturer in Education)

One way in which you can become more critical in your thinking is to use strategies for examining a statement that someone makes or one you read. Four strategies are commonly used:

- setting up comparisons
- questioning the truth of a proposition
- checking the validity of an argument
- pinpointing generalization and assumption

Each of these will be discussed in turn.

## SETTING UP COMPARISONS

**Ask yourself:   Are there different views to be found?**

If we are to think critically, we need to look for a variety of views and compare their strengths and weaknesses. Suppose someone made the statement 'Intelligence is not enough for study because you need motivation.' You might instinctively agree or disagree. A key strategy is that of noting your instinctive reaction. If you say

'That's rubbish', ask yourself why you *instinctively* take that view. You will possibly find that it conflicts with a belief you hold and you can profitably find reasons why you hold to that belief. Try finding reasons why anyone might take a different view from yours because belief and personal opinion are not enough. You need to provide reasons so that you can sustain an academic argument.

A well-tried way to set up comparisons is by looking for differences over a period of time. If there is a change in government policy concerning hospital treatment, for example, you can set up comparisons by asking 'What was treatment like before?', 'What is it like now?' and 'What might it be like in the future?' In higher order questioning you need to develop this technique to compare the meaning and 'significance' of what you encounter. This involves making judgements about the importance or status of one view relative to another. Are there implications for future funding, for example? Why are these implications important and for whom?

Questions like these are rather contrived compared with more spontaneous comparisons which we make. Yet to develop the habit of questioning more spontaneously it may be necessary first to set up comparisons quite deliberately. Once the habit becomes more ingrained, you may find yourself comparing spontaneously as soon as two views, two objects, two policies or two of anything become your focus of attention. Deliberately setting up comparisons reflects the way in which many students already question what they find. Your experience of study at school may confirm this, especially if you are familiar with the concept of 'negative comparison'. Professor E. C. Wragg of Exeter University tells of a school teacher trying to teach children about their topic of 'Insects'. Instead of asking the children 'Who can tell me the name of an insect?', the teacher posed the question 'Why is a bird not an insect?'; in turn this raised further questions about the characteristics of insects, how many legs an insect has, and what different kinds of insects there were. Like many questions that compare two definitions or two concepts, the teacher asked it as an efficient and very effective way of finding out as much information as possible about insects. The example illustrates the ways in which 'Why?' and 'How?' questions can usefully be turned into 'Why not?' and 'How not?' This device can be used to generate more profound questions such as 'How and why isn't evidence opinion?', or 'Why is opinion not necessarily truth?' Positive comparisons explore similarities. Negative comparisons can explore differences, but the aim is still the same: to extend, develop and understand such concepts as 'truth', 'evidence' and 'opinion'. Comparisons are also made to encourage students to refine their definitions.

Higher order questions frequently explore abstract ideas. Questions like 'What is free will?' or 'Does God exist?' contemplate conceptual levels that need efforts of imagination and visualization before we can discuss them. Anything that might be said about higher order questions cannot ignore the point that some study, by its nature, is already of a high conceptual level. Besides this, the more meanings that are compared, the more we are likely to discover that a simple question can lead to issues that are both comprehensive and profound. As soon as we consider another point of view, we are really asking 'How does this change existing points of view?' and 'What similarities and differences are there now?' For example:

> I give my students a poem that I think they've never seen before. We discuss it and then I change the viewpoint. I ask 'Does it make any difference to the poem if I tell you it was written by an American?', 'Does it make any difference if I tell you she was a woman?' . . . 'Does it change things if I tell you she was a black slave?'
>
> (Professor of English and American Studies)

The technique here is to change one aspect of the context and see how it affects views already established in your mind. So far I have suggested that you set up comparisons, to which I would add that you need to be aware of the context in which views are held. The following strategy is not perfect but you may find it useful for writing or discussing:

- Find a viewpoint.
- Test it against alternative views.
- Identify areas of similarity and difference.
- Discuss any issues this raises.
- Ask further questions.
- Speculate on how things might be in a different context.
- Make your comparisons comprehensive.
- Draw some conclusions if you can.

## QUESTIONING THE TRUTH OF A PROPOSITION

**Ask yourself:    Under what circumstances might this be true or false?**

Statements are rarely true or false. Some statements are accepted as true, such as $2 + 2 = 4$, but many statements depend on evidence to support their truth. Question the extent to which something might be true, because there are very few things that are true in all circumstances. If you doubt that, consider what you mean when you describe yesterday's news as being 'old'.

Why would you want to question the truth of a proposition? For that matter, why would you want to know what a proposition is and what it does? The short answer is that questioning a proposition identifies assumptions and raises issues likely to further your understanding. This is not the only way to raise questions and identify significant issues, but it is nevertheless a useful device. A proposition can be examined to see if it might be substantiated. One way to do this is to take up extreme positions and try to argue for and against them. For example, suppose you said 'Most degree courses no longer have final examinations, preferring a mixture of coursework and several minor examinations.' You could take up extremes by trying to substantiate the following propositions:

*Coursework is the most accurate indicator of a student's ability*
*Examinations are the best indicator of a student's ability*

These propositions do not mirror one another exactly. I have deliberately used the words 'best' and 'accurate' rather than their opposites (least accurate and worst). Is accurate therefore the same as best? Wherever you find there is a statement that is a point of view, it is likely to be a proposition and may be followed by questions, argument, reasons and evidence. But nuances of meaning will need to be established as you substantiate your propositions. 'Best' in what sense? 'Accurate' in what sense?

In practice, students do not consciously spend time identifying propositions and labelling them as such. However, if you want to find out if your work has degenerated into bland, rather than meaningful, description, try looking for sentences which are propositions. If there is nothing which might be called into question, it is unlikely that you have propositions forming an argument or a point of view.

The primary characteristic of propositions is that of being true or false (Flew 1975: 10). Higher order questions are therefore those that arise from trying to examine the truth of the proposition. 'Is it true?', 'Where's the evidence?' and 'What are the implications?' are all questions which can be developed to examine a proposition. My strategy for questioning now looks like this (though you will need to devise your own version):

- Why might this proposition be true/false?
- Where is the evidence?
- What assumptions underlie the proposition?
- Are they acceptable assumptions?
- What issues are raised?
- What further questions might be asked?
- Where are there similarities and differences?
- What further issues do these raise?
- How relevant is this to my study/argument?
- What are the implications?
- What propositions might be better ones?
- What conclusions can be drawn?

A question can help to clarify the meaning of a proposition. For instance, suppose you wanted to test to see how well children could read. You might put your trust in a score sheet that included 'number of words not known' or 'number of words misread'. There would be no difficulty coping with the factual statement 'This child misread 17 words', even if you were less happy with the proposition 'This is a good test of reading'. The latter proposition turned into a question could be 'Why is this not a good test of reading?' or 'How is this a good test of reading?', setting you off to find evidence and evaluate assumptions underlying the proposition.

If you wanted to examine whether a proposition was true, a first step would be to try deliberately to argue that it was false. Key questions which might be asked from the above list are 'What assumptions underlie this proposition?' and 'Are they acceptable assumptions?' If they are not acceptable there is bound to be an issue raising yet more questions. Suppose your task was to question the assumptions that might underlie the following controversial propositions. They are taken from *The Harvest of a Quiet Eye* (Mackay 1977).

An intellectual is a parasite that exudes culture.

A committee is a cul-de-sac down which ideas are lured and then quietly strangled.

A great truth is a truth whose opposite is also a great truth.

Provocative propositions, such as the three quoted here, raise issues because they contain assumptions about the meaning of such words as 'parasite' and 'intellectual'. The three propositions are entertaining definitions of 'intellectual', 'committee' and 'great truth'. The proposition 'An intellectual is a parasite that exudes culture' leaves out the context in which it might be true or false. We have to fill in the missing pieces with our own beliefs because we do not know under what circumstances an intellectual (undefined) would be a parasite (undefined). Parasite and intellectual are both loaded words that invite prejudice. As a proposition, it is likely to find different favour among those who do or do not profess to be intellectual. An assumption made is that there is an acceptable link between 'intellectual', 'parasite' and 'culture', even though none of these terms has yet been given meaning.

If propositions can generate questions, so can questions be turned into propositions. This is one useful way to create essay topics. For example, a question like 'Should decisions be made by people who do not have to live with the consequences?' can become a controversial proposition by turning the words around to read: 'Decisions should never be made by people who do not have to live with the consequences.' As a proposition, it is useful as a way to raise further questions so long as we do not accept it at face value. In the form of a *proposition* it may offer a better opportunity for discussion and analysis of issues than it does as a *question*. You may be familiar with public examination papers where, instead of being given an examination question, you are given a proposition and asked to discuss it. The aim is to find a means of allowing you the best opportunity to write.

Apart from changing the wording of questions, four questions in particular are useful for generating propositions. These employ the words 'must', 'should', 'can't' and 'shouldn't'. Their purpose is to take your thinking to extremes and encourage judgement by raising questions:

- What *must* we do about . . . (poverty, terrorism)?
- What *should* we do about . . . (poverty, terrorism)?
- What *can't* we do about . . . (poverty, terrorism)?

- *What shouldn't* we do about (poverty, terrorism)?

Propositions generated from these might be:

Poverty is the responsibility of government.

We cannot eradicate poverty.

Poverty should not be ignored.

Taxes should not be raised to reduce poverty.

I do not propose to raise further questions from these four propositions, though you might wish to spend a few moments to see if you are able to substantiate any as true or false.

### Ask yourself:   Do we need more evidence?

Sometimes higher order thinking is abandoned when we reach conclusions based on insufficient evidence or weak evidence. An example would be survey research using questionnaires, where a very poor response can mean that only the keenest of respondents replied. There are numerous other examples where so much is missing from the supporting evidence or argument that conclusions are impossible to make. You may not know how strong your evidence is until you have spent longer looking at it. An obvious strategy is to suspend judgement and look for stronger evidence or better reasons before drawing conclusions.

## CHECKING THE VALIDITY OF AN ARGUMENT

### Ask yourself:   Are there contradictions?

Being consistent is a fundamental ideal of successful study. Examine whether you are saying the same thing or drifting towards a contradiction. For example, you cannot say that playing the French horn is very difficult to do if you then go on to tell us how easy it would be to learn to play one.

### Ask yourself:   Is this argument allowable, permissible and, if so, why?

If you wanted to assert or deny the truth of your views, you could advance a valid argument that would lead logically to a conclusion or conclusions. However, it is important not to confuse 'validity' with 'truth' or to confuse 'argument' with 'propositions'. There is a straightforward rule for knowing the difference.

- Propositions can be true or false.
- Arguments are valid or invalid.

Philosophers regard this distinction as part of the basic equipment for thinking (Flew 1975: 9). Every fundamental notion in philosophy is sorted by understanding the difference between questions about truth and those that are about validity. According to Flew, we can test a proposition only to see if it is true or false. It is never valid or invalid. Arguments are either valid or invalid and arguments will contain propositions. Validity is not dependent on there being any truth whatever in the propositions that form the constituent parts of an argument. (Valid arguments can contain false or true propositions because valid refers to how permissible or legal the *argument* is.)

Pateman (1987: 1), when discussing philosophy, points out that as a discipline it is seldom about answers and frequently about questions. Philosophy is more concerned with 'good' and 'bad' arguments, and examples in philosophy are provided to illustrate the argument. In philosophy, if you do not follow the argument you will not see the point of the example. An argument of the kind that might be used in an essay or a dissertation would rarely be one which is confined to a few logical lines. In long essays and dissertations, the writing may sustain an overall strategic argument by threading together various supporting points, references and evidence. Here, however, I am concerned with the nuts and bolts of short arguments which might be used along with other material to construct a valid point of view. A more extensive explanation of the development of 'argument' can be found in Chapters 9 and 10.

For an argument to be valid, the various pieces must fit together regardless of whether or not each proposition is true or false. In other words, there should be a logical relationship between the propositions and the conclusion. In the following example, it is the validity of the argument which matters.

There is absolutely no danger from killer bees. You are in more danger from house flies that tread poison across your food. A blue-bottle killed my aunt. She was swatting it when she fell out of the window.

(*The News Quiz*, BBC Radio 4, 1990)

If you were to say that the argument used here is not valid, this would need to be supported by reasons based on your understanding of the argument's flawed logic. There are two propositions (the first two sentences) and two statements, presented as being factual. The first sentence is a proposition which leads to the second proposition. The third sentence is a statement which relates to the conclusion. Yet, as presented to you here, the first three sentences are logically related to each other and we expect the fourth sentence to follow the logic of an aunt dying of 'food poisoning' (inferred from the previous two propositions).

A further word often used in analysing an argument is 'premise' (a proposition or statement from which something else can be inferred). The proposition 'There is absolutely no danger from killer bees' is actually a premise on which the argument is based. The writer implies that we are in more danger from poison carried by house flies. We then assume we are talking about death resulting from food poisoning. Only when we reach the conclusion do we realize that our assumption is false. We can no longer argue that flies are more dangerous than killer bees. Death resulted from falling out of a window.

If an argument is not valid, it is because propositions have been stated without there being a logical connection with the conclusion. This is also true for much more extensive argument such as you might use in an essay or dissertation. Unless you question propositions, or unless they are part of a valid argument which has a logical conclusion, you are likely to receive comments on your essay such as these:

> You have made a number of reasonable assertions which do not constitute an argument. They may be true, but how do we know? Unless you can substantiate them, and argue your case, they remain uninformed and a matter of opinion. Where are your reasons?

You might not accept the original premise 'There is no danger from killer bees', in which case you would reject the whole argument. This would be to dismiss the argument regardless of whether or not it was valid. The premise was false in the first place and the argument which followed has no empirical import. Rejecting the original premise is a favourite device for discarding someone else's argument.

You can be sceptical about all premises, and there are also a number of questions which you can ask yourself about the status of any premise. Is the premise merely an assumption or is there evidence to suggest that it is more substantial than that? Is it prejudice? Is it anecdote, folklore, gossip or opinion? Is it based on sound social or natural science? These are questions that might be asked of your premise before it can be accepted as being reasonable. For example, it is possible to argue that the following premises are of different status. Their significance, value, substance and credibility is not self-evident, but depends on the context in which you argue them.

- Politicians are biased.
- All frogs have two legs.
- Brown eggs are better than white eggs.
- I think, therefore I am.

Few lecturers (with the exception of philosophers and linguists) are likely to ask you to analyse the structure of arguments into constituent parts. Although you need to ask 'What is the status or truth of this statement?', you are not really in the business of analysing the difference between propositions, statements, assertions and premises. You might need to use these terms from time to time, but your central concern is to identify assumptions and go on to argue in a rigorous way.

### Ask yourself: Are there stereotypes here?

A frequent source of distortion in thinking, and one which will destroy your argument, is to resort to stereotypes. This is readily exemplified where people are assumed to be the same because of outward appearance or behaviour. They may wear a uniform, such as in the police or armed services. There are group stereotypes of students being irresponsible, drug-abusing and lazy. The stereotype acts as a bias influencing evidence. Watch out for key phrases such as 'All police . . .'; 'All students . . .'. It is said that racism begins with the stereotype and racist argument then reinforces it. The argument you put forward in an essay needs to be examined closely to see if you are relying on stereotypes rather than evidence.

## PINPOINTING GENERALIZATION AND ASSUMPTION

### Ask yourself: What is being taken for granted here?

Not all generalizations are sweeping and inaccurate. Some generalizations function as a broad summary of truths and evidence you have already put forward. Widely held beliefs, such as 'Pollution destroys the planet', take for granted what we might describe as publicly digested scientific evidence. Assumptions (which I define as *whatever is taken for granted*) are not automatically in themselves a sign of poor academic argument, unless they prove to be false assumptions. We make assumptions every day, based on previous experience. A red traffic light signals 'stop' and we assume drivers will obey the signal. Scientists frequently start with an assumption which they then proceed to test for accuracy. Otherwise, it would not be possible to evolve scientific theories and hypotheses.

In academic discussion and writing, you will inevitably be encouraged to make your points specific rather than general and relevant instead of irrelevant. To do that, you need to identify where you have been generalizing. Without moving from the general to the specific, it becomes very difficult to construct a well-reasoned point of view. A simple device for testing whether or not you have made a generalization is to ask yourself: 'Does what I have just said make me see everyday objects like sticks, stones, tables, chairs, people or animals?' If you cannot picture a situation where you can find everyday objects and actions coming to mind, you may be dealing in abstract generalizations.

Generalizations by their nature are less likely to spark pictures in the mind. An added danger of generalizing is that stereotypes emerge to make the generalization fit a variety of circumstances. People or data that do not fit are simply ignored. Generalizations which are summaries can sometimes be made easier to understand once we add a few details to set them in context. Here is a generalization of sweeping proportions:

*Generalization:*

For every statement there are a thousand contradictions.

To test this generalization we must add our own detail. When we are aware of a context, the generalization becomes less sweeping, but still needs examples and evidence to support it.

*Generalization:*

For every statement that you could make about India there are a thousand contradictions.

Once the words 'about India' are added, the generalization is a less sweeping one. A generalization such as 'nuclear power is dangerous' may conjure fewer specific pictures in your mind than 'traffic is dangerous', but both are really 'potentially' dangerous and therefore the generalization is true only in certain circumstances. If you have no specific context, you can refer only to your own experience. 'Foreigners cannot be trusted' is a similar sweeping generalization because there is plenty of specific evidence to contradict it. The assumption is that all foreigners cannot be trusted. If, however, you engaged in research and gathered data about traffic or nuclear power, it might be possible to make a sound generalization based on the evidence you collected. This would not be an unsupported or 'sweeping' generalization, but would refer to truths drawn from valid argument. Most important of all, you would have set it in an appropriate context. (Many academic papers follow this format, first setting the context and next constructing an argument which takes nothing for granted.)

Propositions occasionally contain assumptions which are expressly designed to provoke a reaction. The motive for making statements like the following is to make you question them. I am using simple examples here, but the strategy which follows can be applied to more sophisticated propositions.

You're an artist, so you'll want a room with the north light.

You've been here a week, so you must know where the fire extinguishers are.

You're a vegetarian, so you must like animals.

What is being taken for granted? There is an assumed relationship between cause and effect. In the middle of each sentence you could write 'so I assume'. The statement then becomes 'You're a vegetarian, so I assume you like animals.' You might reply by saying 'The reason I'm a vegetarian is that I hate animals so much, I couldn't have anything to do with them.' The strategy used is to ask:

- Are these assumptions reasonable?
- Can I believe in them?
- Where's the evidence?

You cannot identify all assumptions by adding the words 'so I assume', because these words do not fit the sense of every sentence containing an assumption. A much easier way to identify a hidden assumption is simply to ask 'Why?' Additionally, as I pointed out at the beginning of this chapter, asking 'Why?' can be a form of higher order questioning in itself. For example, you might have asked a question such as 'How can I advertise cable television?', which omits the question 'Why do I need to advertise cable television in the first place?' The assumption made is that advertising cable television is self-evidently a good or necessary thing to do.

In summary, your strategy for developing higher order questions can be identified as an extension of questions you no doubt already ask. The following are drawn from the main points in the chapter:

- Where/how can comparisons be made?
- What is the significance or status of these?
- What questions might be implied by the text?
- What are the alternative views?
- Are these propositions true? To what extent?
- Why is this proposition not acceptable?
- What assumptions are being made?
- Are they reasonable?
- Is this argument valid?
- Do we need more evidence?
- Are there contradictions?
- Are there better propositions?
- What must/should/can't/shouldn't we do about it?
- How can this generalization be made more specific?

How relevant is all this to your study? I have claimed that higher order questions are also your answers, provided that you ask enough of them and are searching in your attempted answers. If you perceive asking questions as a good way to clarify your thinking, then of course asking questions does give you answers of a sort. In studying for a degree, the basic equipment for thinking must be developed from personal inquiry that includes a healthy scepticism regarding answers to questions. You may not necessarily feel obliged to analyse statements into propositions, assumptions and generalizations, but knowing of strategies to raise higher order questions can, in itself, sharpen your thinking.

**CHECK LIST SUMMARY**

- Plausible propositions in themselves are not evidence or argument.
- When there is an element of doubt there is likely to be an issue.

- A useful way to find an issue is not to accept the proposition as being true.
- If the assumptions underlying a proposition are not reasonable, then there are bound to be issues.
- A viewpoint cannot be substantiated without its being thoroughly questioned in the first place to establish meaning.
- Propositions can be true or false.
- Arguments can be valid or invalid.
- A proposition can be made expressly with the purpose of provoking a reaction.
- Stereotypes distort an argument.
- Questions containing 'must', 'should', 'can't' or 'shouldn't' can generate propositions.

**ACTION PLAN**

- Find, or devise, a proposition that you can debate.
- Identify the assumption/s.
- Give reasons why the proposition is true or false.
- Check for inconsistencies and contradictions.
- Support propositions with evidence and reasons.
- Find 'Why?' and 'How?' questions. Turn these into negative 'Why not?' and 'How not?' questions.
- Check the validity of your argument.
- Examine implications and draw some conclusions if you can.

# Chapter 5

# Reading academic texts

## SKIMMING IS NOT WHAT IT USED TO BE

In the 1970s speed reading was in vogue and enthusiasts made great claims for techniques that would turn a difficult task into a much easier one. As Gibbs (1977: 111) and other researchers soon found, students who tried these techniques were often quite incapable of understanding what they were reading. The mechanics of reading were inseparable from 'purpose' and, as a result, many students were prone to misorientation. They also began to think that the only way to read text was quickly, sometimes with disastrous results. As we will see, skimming over text in order to take in the content quickly is no guarantee that you will absorb anything meaningful.

> I'm so busy trying to skim the page as fast as I can that I don't remember anything. I keep thinking 'I've got to hurry . . . I must remember this, I must remember that . . .' so I don't remember anything in the end.
>
> (Education student)

> I tend to read the first chapter to see how interesting it is. If it's dull I skim headings to see how relevant the rest might be. I'm not really keen on skim reading because I've found you really have to go back and read it properly anyway.
>
> (Environmental studies student)

If speed reading techniques were such a success, every child in school would be taught speed reading as a matter of habit. This does not happen. Students read academic books with various purposes in mind and reading at speed can sometimes be a hindrance rather than a help. On the other hand, slow reading also has its disadvantages.

I've found that if I read too slowly I get stuck on particular passages and don't pick out the main points. I found that by reading fairly quickly, at least at first, I carry the main points in my head and immediately start to select what I want. This is especially useful when you're reading long documents, as I have to.

(Law student)

Skimming is a well-tried way to see if the book is relevant or not. Of course, it has limitations. You can skim to find out whether or not you are dealing with such material as information, argument or description, but not to extract deeper meaning. For that there is no substitute for careful reading that allows you time to think and question.

An argument often put forward in favour of skimming a chapter is that skimming prevents the reader isolating the difficult parts of the text and studying them out of context. If you have ever tried to learn to play a musical instrument, like the piano, you will know that the first page of a piece of music usually has much more of your attention. You probably insist on correcting every mistake before continuing. The same applies to a complicated piece of text. Skimming reinforces your overview of the text so that difficult passages are at least put in context.

The text of some academic books is often so dense that to abandon skimming and start at the first page and try to understand every word will take you little further than page three. This is especially true if your approach to a book is to memorize what you have read. Marton, Hounsell and Entwistle (1984) drew a clear distinction between those students who wanted to be able to repeat parts of what they had read verbatim and those who gave a variety of reinterpretations of the text. They found that trying to memorize text resulted in a qualitatively poorer grasp of meaning than trying to find out what the author was saying. This has distinct parallels with the 'having' and 'being' modes of learning described in Chapter 2. In reading text, 'having' is about remembering every word and 'being' is about understanding. Your motive for reading may lead you to one of these two possibilities:

- To learn the text
- To learn *from* the text

Postgraduate students I have interviewed say that they are already very familiar with reading techniques picked up at school or university. On one point they are unanimous: how they will read depends on what they are reading and why they are reading it. Research documented in the 1980s reveals very few surprises on this matter. We all read and study in different ways at different times. I cannot imagine skimming a poem to discover its contents nor would I necessarily start at the first page of an academic textbook. The spectrum of approaches is likely to run from information seeking, which is like using a telephone directory, to reading a novel or a poem where the unfolding of a particular sequence of words matters. As one student commented, 'Skimming a chapter can be a complete waste of time if it's full of jargon or the content is boring. You'd have to read it properly anyway in the end.'

You may not be the world's fastest reader, but experimenting a little with reading speed can pay off. Although it takes time to see words on a page, you stand a better chance of remembering the first half of a sentence if you read quickly enough to reach the second half. As Frank Smith (1971: 46–8) explains, if you read too slowly, your short-term memory does not retain information and meaning. Short-term memory can, in any case, retain only about half a dozen items at any one time. Three or four eye movements per second is about the average reading scan and by reading slightly more quickly, some readers can take in more words than others. The least efficient way to read is to try to understand every single word before you reach the end of a sentence (Buzan 1974: 31). The reason for this is that we need far more clues for meaning than we receive word by word. Reading slightly faster may encourage you to retain more meaning if you are a slow reader, but you can only try this for yourself to see how effective it is.

One popular technique is to look for signals in the first lines of paragraphs such as 'In summary', 'First of all', 'Finally' or 'By contrast'. Reading the first lines of each paragraph can sometimes give an indication of the topic being dealt with in the full paragraph. These signals often show the structure of a passage of text and you can use them to grasp the gist and layout of what you are about to read. Rowntree (1988: 102–3) called these 'verbal signposts' and gave such examples as 'Now we come to an aspect that may seem surprising', 'For instance', and 'At this point the argument becomes involved'. These are all pauses in the text to point out to the reader what has just been said, what is about to come, or what is about to be further explained. They signal structure and turning points in a chapter.

## KNOWING WHY YOU READ CONDITIONS HOW YOU READ

Centuries ago, students went up to Oxford or Cambridge to read for a degree. The tradition of 'reading for a degree' arose because there were few academic books, apart from those held by these two great universities. Student and teacher would read and translate their classics together. If you wanted to read for a degree, you went to Oxford or Cambridge because that was where the books were kept. Reading for your degree still makes some sense. Lecturers will talk of 'reading around the subject' and expect you to develop a much wider view than they can give you through lectures. One obvious reason for reading is to find material that feeds into an essay, discussion, seminar or assignment. You are looking for useful material, some of which might be quoted in support of your points. Another is to compare alternative views. A third is to read two versions of the same topic to understand ideas more comprehensively.

You may have no choice. Some lecturers punctuate their courses with 'reading tasks' and expect you to respond in a seminar to a particular chapter or paper. They do not expect you merely to read, but to gain something from the process. What you gain will rarely coincide exactly with other students' gains because we often read expecting the text to confirm or change what we already bring to it (see Säljö in Marton *et al.* 1984: 71–89). Consequently, your own views may prevent you from understanding, add additional meanings, or unduly emphasize certain passages in the text. What you derive from reading may depend on how prepared you are to consider views that clash with your own.

More important still is the extent to which learning habits can limit the way in which we read. If our assumptions about learning lead us to see text as being 'useful information', then that is how we will approach reading it. If we are in search of 'issues', we will most likely find them. If we need to memorize a list of facts, we will search for facts; and if we want to discover the author's main viewpoint, we will look for that. One student might be able to describe the sequence of a particular chapter. Another student might extract the main issues or processes, but does not know in which order they come. Both might have read something worthwhile, but their perspectives would lead them to a different understanding of the same text.

For most of us there are two possible starting points for reading anything academic, these being 'searching' and 'browsing'. We might already be searching through books for a particular topic or some information, in which case we are likely to select and reject by flipping through pages to plunder the contents. Alternatively, we might pick up a book and browse through it to see if anything catches our eye. Either strategy can still be analytical and rigorous, but our motive would determine what we found. Here is one reason for reading books relevant to studying for a higher degree.

First of all, to survive a PhD you can't get away without doing a lot of reading. Most reading I did was to find out how one writer's views differed from another . . . some of the books made similar points to my own research, but I was anxious to find out where the differences were. The philosophy of the subject was important too because for a PhD you have to develop your own philosophy and principles to put your work in an acceptable context. You have to know about different philosophies before you can begin to write about your own.

(PhD student)

You might not be ready to tackle a PhD, but the principle still applies. If you write essays which are full of opinions that clearly have no basis in background reading, your lecturers are likely to detect this very quickly. There is 'opinion' and 'informed opinion' that you gain through reading. Essays do not always need to be punctuated with quotations and full of bracketed references to be well argued. But you are unlikely to be convincing if you have no alternative views to discuss, or have not gained a good grasp of the main issues. This is not exactly a high ideal, more a way of life when you study for a degree. You read to clarify your own thinking and broaden your understanding of your chosen subject. Often one book will lead you to discover another. PhD students, for example, find that reading a quotation or a reference in one book frequently leads them to read another ten books which they found quoted.

If you are a 'searcher', you already think you know what you want from a book or paper. You are looking for headings and content that coincides with your needs, usually to write an essay or a dissertation. Though 'searching' is an understandable activity, it carries the penalty that you might miss other passages of useful and interesting text. As the previous chapters suggested, you may have posed questions which you are trying to answer as you are reading.

If you are a 'browser' as well as a 'searcher', you are prepared to be side-tracked by material if it seems interesting. Maybe you have not tied yourself too strictly to the task of reading only the material that immediately strikes itself as necessary for your study. You find that reading alternative views is very stimulating, despite the time it takes.

## ACADEMIC WRITING STYLE CAN SLOW DOWN YOUR READING

If you are a student new to degree work, books on the reading list can be a shock to the system. Sometimes the academic style of them is daunting and you may wonder why on earth they are written as they are. Many books are so specialized that they seem full of jargon for the new reader. Every degree subject develops its own specialist vocabulary which some readers perceive as jargon, even though an author may not think so. Computer studies are rife with phrases such as 'transputed parallel processing' and sociology went through a phase in the 1970s when the use of jargon seemed to be generated out of all proportion to the content. Academic writing has always had its share of this, but there are other reasons why text proves difficult to read. Knowing some of them is not going to change the text, but it may help you to cling on rather than give up trying to understand difficult passages of writing. I have identified six common difficulties here:

- too much jargon
- many references
- very abstract ideas
- long sentences
- few analogies or examples
- passive voice used to excess

Jargon, in my view, is nothing more than a shorthand that attempts (eventually) to speed up the pace at which you understand. Jargon words and phrases categorize, specialize and make official rather complex or vague ideas. Confusion arises because jargon signals huge chunks of information to those who happen to be 'in the know'. It is a shorthand that has to be learned and assimilated. Too much jargon per page is irritating and you may feel that all you can do is to let it pass you by. That is exactly what children do when they do not understand words or what you might do if you were listening to a foreign language, only half of which you understood. Since you are unlikely to be given a translation, your strategy at first is to let jargon pass you by and continue reading.

In many academic papers, you are likely to find that writers justify almost every statement with references to previous research or authoritative sources. The style of an academic paper, or monograph, merits this treatment because papers tend to be written bearing in mind other academics who are certain to know literature in the field. (This point will be amplified in Chapters 6, 8 and 9 on essay and dissertation writing.) You will find that references appearing throughout the text inevitably slow down your reading and disturb the flow. They often contribute to boredom and all you can do is to ignore the assorted brackets and move swiftly on, or read slowly and thoughtfully. Here, as an example, are two versions of the same text. Although it is easier to pick up the sense of the second version, a researcher would need the references shown in the first version. If you are new to study, you are about to come across a great deal of academic referencing and you may as well try to familiarize yourself with seeing it.

> Tyler (1949) and other evaluators have tried to define evaluation. As David Nevo (1986) pointed out: There is consensus regarding the definition of the evaluation as the assessment of merit or worth (Eisner 1979; Glass 1969; House 1980; Scriven 1967; Stufflebeam 1974) or as an activity comprised of both description and judgement (Guba and Lincoln 1981; Stake 1967).
>
> (*Cambridge Journal* 1988)

> Tyler and other evaluators have tried to define evaluation. They agree about the definition of evaluation as the assessment of merit or worth; or as an activity comprised of both description and judgement.

Justification, by reference to another authority, can be convincing. Brackets and semi-colons signal a wealth of agreement and evidence about the points being made. The quality of research being used to support your points is, of course, not indicated, so the reader actually takes a great deal on trust. Those academics who are familiar with the specialism being written about will know many of the references and will know that the practice of justifying text with references is not foolproof. Using statistics to support a case can be even more convincing than giving references in brackets, and here it is easy to become cynical about the whole business of referencing. Dr John Collee made a wry comment on this:

> Numbers in medicine still have a magical significance. In Clement VI's time, physicians generally chose simple numbers (six serpents in your belly, four evil humours, 13 demons in your spine . . .) Nowadays we spray complex statistics around for effect, but the intention is the same, to generate belief.
>
> (*The Observer*, 10 November 1990)

Sometimes the material you are trying to read holds you back because it is abstract. The topic it deals with is difficult in itself and contains few concrete examples to illustrate the abstractions. Apart from being abstract, it may contain so many long sentences, or commas, or even sub-clauses, extra details that lose the thread of the beginning of the sentence, additional sub-clauses attempting to creep in, often with irrelevant asides, punctuated with cross references, so that you need to read it repeatedly before you can understand it (with additional comment added in brackets for extra turgid and boring text) and you become confused, assuming you are still able to concentrate. Qualifying phrases, such as 'Although I have said material can be abstract', slow down the pace at which you can take in the real point of the sentence. The crux of the meaning comes too late. Philosophy is a discipline which is prone to long sentences because philosophical ideas, by their nature, can be abstract and complicated. Philosophers want to be quite sure they have covered every eventuality when they construct a sentence.

The problem for many readers is that it is very difficult to keep the first part of a long philosophical sentence in their heads while reading the remainder. Where a writer uses a complex argument we need very powerful examples to set the context. We can see just how abstract text can be in the following piece (admittedly quoted out of context) from *Thinking about Thinking* by Antony Flew:

> When we say that p is a logically sufficient condition of q, then we are saying that we could not assert p and deny q without contradicting ourselves. But when such and such is said to be not the logical, but the causally sufficient condition of this or that, then it is being said that, in the world as it actually is, with

the laws of nature what they actually are, such and such could not in fact be produced without producing this or that.

(Flew 1975: 40–1)

Too many this's or that's? Maybe there are too few concrete examples or analogies for us to recognize when we lift text from its surrounding paragraphs. Whenever ideas seem complicated, we need considerable courage to stay with them and read the passage of text again. A combination of long sentences, jargon and abstraction can make reading very tedious indeed. All the more reason to concentrate on a mental map which overviews the entire context.

As if abstract ideas were not difficult enough, academic papers and official documents such as solicitors' contracts are rife with the use of the 'passive voice'. Here are some typical translations:

*Passive:* You are expected to remain in your seats please.
*Active:*  Please stay in your seats.

*Passive:* The family car has been stolen and it has been wrecked.
*Active:*  A thief stole the family car and wrecked it.

*Passive:* The assumption is made intentionally.
*Active:*  The assumption is intentional.

*Passive:* If you were asked.
*Active:*  If anyone asked you.

The effect of using passive voice is to make writing seem long-winded and difficult to read. Perhaps it is the academics' need to sound objective and distanced from the evidence they have collected that encourages this form of sentence. A reader of average ability will find text heavy-going if there is more than about 15 per cent passive voice according to established formulae such as the long-established Flesch readability procedure of 1951. (Flesch readability is not without its problems as a measure, but is relevant to the point made here.) Insurance policies and legal documents are usually way above this percentage in their use of passive voice. The passive voice, which is apparently the last tense to be understood by overseas students, is impersonal, distanced and wordy. Sometimes it is essential. Legal documents probably use the 'passive voice' to remove personal responsibility from the lawyer and transfer sentences to the cold climate of the law courts. Scientific papers in particular exemplify a style that tries to make evidence sound objective by using the passive voice. You cannot do anything about text that is passive, but knowing about it may help you to hang in there and keep going.

## SOME WELL-TRIED PRACTICAL READING TECHNIQUES

Trying to come to grips with a particular book which forms the basis of your course is very different from plundering the library shelves in preparation for writing an essay. A panic-stricken plunder will no doubt find you searching for sentences to quote and discuss. The techniques which I include here are those that researchers and students have found useful since study techniques became part of many degree courses. Of course, if you want to read in an active way, you must be prepared to question as you read, rather as if you were one of the world's sceptics. The following examples assume there are some course books which you want to understand more fully, rather than relying on looting the index of a dozen others. Here are six examples:

- touring a book
- underlines and highlights
- making a map
- asking questions
- making comparisons
- reviewing

Any study book can be toured in an efficient sequence, but some starting points are better than others. Your aim is to gain the best insight into a book's content in the shortest possible time. For example, the shortest summary of a book will usually appear as the 'blurb' on its outside cover or flyleaf. The blurb is partly an advertising device to sell books, but also tells you why you should read the book. A library book may have been rebound or lost its paper cover so the blurb is missing, but if one is there, read it carefully. Doing so may tell you enough to put the book back where it came from without going any further.

Some students quite deliberately make their next step either looking at the contents listing, reading the introduction, or looking at the conclusions (if there are any). These are mental maps for finding your way around the book. Once past the blurb and contents, you might flip through pages in various ways avoiding detailed reading. Resisting the urge to read a specific section, you might next glance at all the remaining pages to give yourself a good grasp of the book's layout. A useful rule of thumb for this, in my experience, is to turn every page from start to finish allowing about one second per page, perhaps pausing here and there. Sometimes this is worth doing twice so that you know the location of sections of text. Not everything will be headed as clearly as 'conclusions' or 'summary'. Even so, allowing yourself a second or two for each page can reveal concluding paragraphs that summarize or pull forward the main points made. The general aim is to do this until you are quite sure where to find things by knowing what is the layout of the contents.

Several research projects (Blanchard and Mikkelson 1987; Idstein and Jenkins 1972) show that using an author's headings, or underlining passages in pencil, helps you to remember the structure of a chapter. This is another way to construct a mental map of the text. Provided the book is your own, you are free to underline text and highlight as you wish. Remember, however, that you may later disagree with your own emphasis of the text and wish you had never underlined anything. If the book belongs to a library, or to someone else, there is no reason that I can think of to justify marking the text. Nothing is more frustrating than to borrow a library book and discover that someone else has underlined the passages that were meaningful for them. If you have already experienced this frustration, you will easily understand my point about bringing your own experience to a piece of text.

As I pointed out in Chapter 3, practising making a map on the back of an envelope helps you to analyse text very quickly. You are primed to look for structures and pull out the main issues rather than drift from paragraph to paragraph. Alternatively, you might have three questions in mind and scan through the pages of a book looking for answers. Searching like this is efficient, but less likely to reveal an author's point of view than reading long sections of text. There is something to be said for allowing the author to speak to you through the structure of the whole book. You might take a more analytical approach and ask yourself 'What are the assumptions underlying this book?' 'Is the text sufficient or are there incomplete sections?' 'Is evidence and opinion merged or is it distinguished one from the other?' Suppose you were studying History, Politics or Education. You might devise a question such as 'How has the distribution of power changed in the last five years and what are the effects on society?' This broad topic would dominate your thoughts as you read and provide a useful peg on which to hang your ideas. It would be up to you to decide how prominently this question featured if you were about to gather ideas for an essay.

In the previous chapter, 'setting up comparisons' came top of my list of ways to ask higher order questions. You will find that similarities and differences between authors' views and your own generate useful material for you. You might also compare to find issues that are contentious ones. Naturally, there are limits to how many questions and comparisons you can keep in your head as you read. Most questions will be in the background. When you compare one book (or paper) with another you may find these strategies suit your purpose:

- comparing writers' assumptions
- comparing similarities and differences
- comparing the overall structures
- comparing the styles of presentation
- comparing conclusions and any recommendations
- devising your own theme or question

Almost every book written about study techniques emphasizes the importance of reviewing or revising notes you make. (Not every student makes notes from books, but most do.) You usually need to evaluate the text you read to see how it fits your understanding and reasons for reading in the first place. When you are trying to remember, possibly for an examination, you function best by reviewing 'mental maps' frequently, rather than leaving them to gather the dust (Buzan 1974; Rowntree 1988; Maddox 1988; Russell 1979). Some students build a collection of bookmarks (see Chapter 3) and others a lever arch file of flow charts. Frequent revision of these summaries is often all that is needed to reinforce understanding as well as memory. You might also discuss ideas with a friend or a fellow student. The aim is to reinforce, revise and develop your understanding of the material that you have read. This goes hand in hand with asking higher order questions (discussed in Chapter 4).

The simplest way to review or revise your reading matter might be to recheck your mental map or 'flyer template' against the text. Most students are not going to make elaborate notes unless they have a very good reason to do so. Your aim is more likely to be one of absorbing and digesting as much of the content as you can, in the hope that you understand it. But can you tell someone else anything about the content, issues and ideas contained in the book? If you made a copy of the structure of a chapter on the back of an envelope, reviewing is often a matter of puzzling over this sketch and trying to recall the details. Techniques for this vary and some students might prefer to return to scanning pages to reinforce the content of the whole book. For those students, a mental map is an impression of scanned pages, supported by the occasional detailed read.

Finally, you might discuss your 'map' with a colleague or try to give a summary of the main points as if you were explaining in an examination or writing an essay. If you are reading in an active way, you are not just enjoying the text for its own sake, but trying to study it. For that you will need to be ready to question, talk and write about the content of what you have read, not just enjoy a good read and hope that something sinks in.

## CHECK LIST SUMMARY

- The mechanics of reading are inseparable from 'purpose'.
- Slow reading also has its disadvantages.
- Learn the text or learn *from* the text?
- Knowing *why* you read conditions *how* you read.
- Touring a book via blurb, contents and skimming.
- Using underlines and highlights.
- Asking questions.
- Making comparisons.
- Reviewing.
- Devising a topic.
- Comparing author's assumptions.
- Comparing differences, similarities, styles and conclusions

## ACTION PLAN

- Discuss your 'map' with a colleague.
- Try to recount the content of a chapter to a critical friend.
- Imagine/devise a question that might appear in an examination paper on the passage of text you have read.
- Recount the chapter to yourself solely from the mental map which you made.

# Chapter 6

# Learning about essays

## MODELS ARE INADEQUATE, STRATEGIES ARE NOT

If you have ever filled in a questionnaire, you will probably know that certain questions do not allow you to answer as you would like. You would prefer to write 'it depends' rather than fill in boxes or put a mark on a five-point scale. Essay models that suggest the best structure to use and exactly how to go about it suffer from a similar defect. You would quite like to use the structure, but it simply will not fit your current essay. Worse still, the advice you follow about essay writing might be fine for a subject like Environmental Science, but what if you are studying Medicine, Law or the Social Sciences?

Students occasionally find their favourite ways to write, however, regardless of the essay topic.

> Well, for me it's a question of defining terms first. Then I go straight to the essay question.
>
> (Economics student)

> The way I tackle assignments is to find a good quote to capture the interest of the reader. Or else I'll make a controversial statement to start off the argument and set the scene. The structure is something I plan very roughly because I don't really know what the structure is until I have written the first draft. Then I modify my original structure and tighten up the points I'm making. If I'm really lucky I'll find a good quote that sums up everything I have said at the end.
>
> (History student)

I suspect that most students believe their essays are structured whether or not they actually are. The material that follows is about elementary, basic essay writing. Although it does not deal with advanced techniques and ideas, the content feeds into Chapters 8 and 9 dealing with dissertation writing. For these chapters, basic essay writing techniques are a foundation.

The trouble with writing essays is that you can think that what you have written is as clear to your lecturer as it is to you. In practice, you might find that you become aware of what you really wanted to say only when your essay is marked or you have a tutorial in which to discuss it. You are quite likely to hand in an essay just at the point where it would be best left for a week so that you could take a fresh look at the way you wrote it. Unless you let someone else read it to see if it makes sense, you are likely to hand it in when you are far too close to your own writing to judge its impact. Given that your essay might confuse its reader, devising a structure for it would seem all the more important. Yet knowing the structure in advance can prove to be an irksome constraint because essays have a way of developing in a direction you least expect. Your original structure is then threatened.

Despite this drawback I believe that starting with an arbitrary 'ghost' structure or outline helps you to organize and communicate your thoughts more effectively. You can always abandon the structure if it does not work. (I use the term 'ghost' to mean an outline that is bound to disappear as the essay begins to demand something more solid.) If you have no structure, it is very difficult to express a point of view and almost impossible to construct a logical argument to support your case. Additionally, if you want your essay to have impact, you will need to make some points more forcibly than others and lend shape to your argument if there is one. You may not like an arbitrary fixed structure, but a ghost structure is one you devise with every intention of changing your ideas.

Some essay titles are chosen by you, not set by your lecturers. Although this is obviously an advantage, at some point in your degree course you will need to develop the discipline of answering set questions and writing to a set topic. In examinations, for example, you will have fewer options open to you and will be disadvantaged if you have no experience of writing set essays. You might argue, of course, that as soon as you decide on an essay title it becomes fixed anyway, so the strategies that underlie your essay writing apply equally to set or chosen titles.

In my experience, there are pitfalls connected with choosing a title and you should be wary. Where you have a free choice, you may well discover that unless you negotiate its exact wording with your lecturer, you may find yourself writing on a topic that offers you very little of substance or is too difficult to tackle. If essay topics are too easy or too difficult to write about, they are usually too difficult to mark, so your lecturer also has an interest in agreeing a good topic with you. More important is the possibility that the essay will be less successful. Negotiating a title should, in my view, prompt you to ask your lecturer: 'Do you think this is a topic worth writing about or should I try something else?' If you are typical, the mistake you will make is to choose an essay topic that is far too wide, or to choose one which lends itself to overlong description. You will more than likely be steered towards a focused and specific essay title:

> If you're looking at historical documents or sorting out your reading, you need to look for issues and things you can question. There has to be something worth writing about and you won't get that by describing a document. You have to look at your evidence and see what it means. For instance, we're looking at the 'Music Hall' as evidence of imperialism . . . so we'll look at the songs and find out what values are embedded in the verses. Then we'll relate those to other evidence from the period.
>
> (Lecturer in History)

You write essays because they teach you something, not just as an exercise to prove you can write. Besides gaining a coursework grade or mark, essay writing clarifies your thinking, gives you some idea of how well you understand the subject, and is therefore an important means of developing your thoughts. The actual process of writing is as important as the end product. That at least is the theory.

## FINDING A FOCUS

Devising questions can help you to find a focus to write about. You might begin by finding a problem, a puzzle, or an issue that intrigues you. Studying History you might wonder, for example, what some Edwardian values such as 'patriotism' meant to people at the time. If you were teaching a foreign language you might be interested in whether certain household objects were more useful than others for the teaching of French. In Politics you might consider how power had shifted between local councils and central government. English Literature might prompt an essay about the portrayal of Shakespeare's *King Lear*. Questions like the following might generate some of your essay material:

**Questions:**

- What did Edwardian values like 'patriotism' mean to people at the time (compared with our understanding of 'patriotism' today)?
- Are some everyday objects more useful than others for the teaching of French?
- How has power shifted from local councils to central government?
- Should Shakespeare's character Lear be played as a fool or a madman?

Alternatively, as I described in Chapter 4, you might want to turn questions into controversial propositions and question these to raise further issues. Your propositions might look something like this and the question they raise is: 'Do I accept the proposition as true or not?'

**Propositions:**

- Edwardian values such as patriotism have as much relevance today as they did years ago.
- Some everyday objects are more useful than others for the teaching of French.
- Central government has legislated against local councils to remove many of their powers.
- Shakespeare intended Lear to be played as a madman.

The most likely aim in discussing these propositions is to explore issues and ensure that your essay remains relevant throughout. Your best intentions can drift towards irrelevance as you become absorbed in reading and gathering material for your essay. Take, for example, a typical essay question for an education student, the kind of question that might also appear in education examinations: 'Discuss the role of the teacher in implementing the Mathematics curriculum.' It does not take much analysis to realize that the question asks you to 'Discuss the *role*'. A trip to the library shelves reveals that they are not exactly bulging with books about role, but they are certainly bulging with books about 'curriculum', 'National Curriculum', and 'Mathematics'. By the time you have digested this material, the issue of role is pushed well into the background. Why has the title asked you to discuss role? Probably, so that you have to take all the material you can find and think your own way through its relationship to 'role'. That is why a lecturer sets an essay title that cannot be tackled by making a collage of pieces extracted from books. If you write an essay about 'curriculum' and you make 'role' a secondary feature, you have plainly missed the point.

The difference between waffle and irrelevance is slight. Irrelevant material can be good material that has found its way into the wrong essay or is in the wrong place. If you are unable to make clear connections between one idea and another, your reader might assume that your material is irrelevant, even if in your eyes it is not. Waffle is meaningless filling or meaningless statements of a very general kind. For example, if I say: 'We must all work together to create a caring society', this means nothing very significant. Most of us would agree, much as we would with statements like: 'Cities would be better places if there were no crimes committed' or 'We must improve our hospitals, schools and provision for the disabled.' These statements are very broad generalizations. If you think you have written waffle, test it, by removing it, to see if your essay survives perfectly well without it.

## GENERATING A CONTEXT FOR YOUR ESSAY

Whether or not your lecturer sets the essay title, you will need to generate a context or background for it. This is not necessarily your starting point when you actually write your essay, but without knowing the context in which you want to set your essay it is even harder to write the opening paragraphs. To set the context you may delve into books and papers, gather research data or look for government reports with which to build up a background picture. Sometimes this is a matter of defining the limitations of your topic or defining your terms. An essay needs to be set within certain understandable parameters and to take account of previous writing on the subject, if there is any. You will find it a good idea to compare conflicting views. You cannot make your points and ignore research or literature in the field if it is relevant, which is precisely why background reading or data gathering is necessary for so many essays. English Literature is sometimes an exception to this because the background reading can be the novel itself, a play or poem rather than literary criticism or documented research.

The context may be discovered as a result of asking yourself questions like these:

- Does the context have a history to it?
- Is the context a particular problem?
- Does the context, for example, concern a law, principle or policy?
- What is essential here for the reader to understand my purpose?
- What reading do I need to do to build the context?
- If I'm looking for evidence to set the context, where is it?
- When does the background material become irrelevant?
- Who has written conflicting views?
- What issues might be included to set the context?

The main source of difficulty in setting a context is that you are likely to *describe* the context rather than weave it in with your introductory issues. Description, as we will see, can be dismally boring to read unless something of interest relieves the gloom. I mention this because the context is likely to be set early on in your essay and you hardly want to alienate your reader at this stage. Description need not always be included without issues being touched on, as the following contrasting examples show.

Over 50 miles of bicycle track were established in the city between 1987 and 1991. Cycle accidents fell by 20 per cent compared with levels across the population as measured in the first half of the decade. This was despite an increase of 10 per cent in volume of traffic.

(issues not signalled)

The call for more cycle tracks within the city is made when the volume of traffic has risen by 10 per cent from 1987–91. The 50 miles of track in use during these years prompted this investigation into why the incidence of cycle accidents dropped by 20 per cent during this period. We can only guess what the likely level of accidents might have been without establishing the cycle track and find out what public reaction is to using more pavement areas for this purpose.

(issues of public reaction, verification of cause and effect, call for more tracks to be established)

So far, I have mentioned various questions you might ask yourself to set the context. I have in mind a student surrounded by documents, books, data and scribbles on notepaper who is probably punch-drunk with assorted reading-matter that might or might not prove useful. One of the most frequently reported effects of reading and researching for an essay is the stage where students are totally confused by random and conflicting material they have read. They might be able to set the context, but where do they go from there? Do they write six major points down and expand on them? Do they assemble their resources in order of importance?

## OPENING PARAGRAPHS

Good starting points are often those that lead the reader into your thoughts about the central issues of the essay topic. Sometimes you will begin by quoting a researcher or writer. Occasionally you will need to define your terms in the first few paragraphs, though this has its problems, mentioned in detail in Chapter 9. Essentially your introduction should say something about how you have decided to structure your essay by such means as dividing it into two, three or four sections. (Some students write their introduction last because they do not know exactly how the essay will be structured until it is in draft form.) Your reader is given a summary route map to help clarify what is to follow. There is, however, a much more fundamental reason for thinking carefully about your introduction.

Writing the introduction is your opportunity to set the intellectual and conceptual level of your essay. Reference to established research or important issues is not compulsory in an introduction, but you do yourself no service by beginning in a way that creates a poor impression. Making reference to writers and researchers has a curiously reassuring effect on some readers who feel more confident that as a writer you have taken notice of other sources of authority from the very beginning. You may not like this convention, but an early reference to serious issues, perhaps with a sideways glance at existing research, does not go amiss if you want to pitch the level of your writing as high as you can. Making essays and dissertations interesting obviously helps, but you need not sacrifice substantial content for fear of boring your reader. Academic essays are usually assessed rather than published. Several cameos of starting points can be identified.

*Rocket launcher* is when you begin with an intriguing issue, launch a few ideas and see where they land. Sometimes you raise a question, but the aim is still to launch your ideas in a way that stimulates your reader to think about the main issues and about your argument.

*Quoter* is the frequently used starting point mentioned at the beginning of this chapter. Be careful about the quotation you choose or the rest of your essay may be constrained by it.

*Promiser* is when you begin your essay by making promises concerning what you are writing about. Openings such as 'This essay discusses/analyses/researches' are all promises that must later be fulfilled. Often it turns out to be very difficult to fulfil the promises you made in your introduction and you have therefore only teased the reader.

*Explainer* is a starting point where you explain a concept or problem before going on to the real business of your essay. This is sometimes a necessary way to begin writing about a complex subject.

*Questioner* is similar to 'rocket launcher' except that you use a question as the means of raising an issue. This can be a successful way to start off except that some readers are irritated by an essay that begins with a question. Additionally, there are inappropriate questions such as 'Have you ever wondered what makes a brain cell different from a liver cell?' Such starting points involve the reader in a way in which they might rather not be involved. You might begin by questioning a proposition as I discussed in Chapter 4.

*Comparison maker* is a technique where you make comparisons from the very beginning of your essay. This is an effective way to make your points, provided you can sustain the comparisons. An example of this would be where an essay compared eastern and western philosophies so that the comparison would almost certainly be signalled in the title. You may decide that comparisons are best left until slightly later in your essay if the title does not suggest them.

*Dictionary buff* is, in my view, one of the least effective starting points. Quite contrary to expectations, a dictionary definition can make for an uncertain beginning by claiming terms are accurately defined when they are really wide open to interpretation. Explicit dictionary definitions have very limited authority when compared with definitions that appear within their appropriate context. (Chapter 9 explains this more fully.) In practice, dictionary definitions have all too brief a meaning for your introduction; more seriously, they cite a published source as if it were beyond question. Some dictionary definitions are listed in a variety of forms from which you are obliged to choose one example. The dictionary definition for 'essay', for instance, is 'a short literary work' in one dictionary, while another says it is 'an attempt: a first effort: a tentative draft'. Dictionary definitions can rarely stand alone at the beginning of your text. You may not agree with the view that defining terms by using a dictionary is a disappointing start to an essay, but there are numerous lecturers for whom dictionary definitions immediately signal superficiality. Definitions of this kind become a straitjacket and are a poor means of establishing what you are about to write.

## WHY WASTE A GOOD QUOTATION?

Students frequently misunderstand the purpose of quotations and references. Finding a really impressive quotation is one thing, but using it well in your essay is quite another matter. It is sometimes better to put quoted material into your own words and acknowledge the source. You need to be quite sure that a quotation is worth using.

Quotations are a form of reference. If you quote something without acknowledging its source and weave it into your own writing it is, of course, plagiarism. Plagiarism is a serious offence and often easier to detect than you might think, especially if the style of your essay suddenly changes. Copying or close paraphrasing of someone else's work is one form of plagiarism. Taking ideas as if they were your own and using them is another form of plagiarism. You might think that there is a wafer-thin distinction between stealing an idea and allowing that idea to spark your own thinking. Ideas, whatever their source, become the 'digested wisdom' within a subject and you will occasionally find yourself using ideas that have their source elsewhere. Yet, because this may still appear to be plagiarism (even if it is not so), it is much safer to acknowledge your source. Lecturers who thoroughly understand their subject will almost certainly know where your ideas came from.

I take the view that there is no such thing as a 'stand-alone' quote, one that appears isolated within the text without any reference to anything that goes before or comes after it. A quotation appears in your text for three main reasons.

- It supports your previous point.
- It sets up a comparison.
- You are about to discuss it analytically.

You may be tempted to include a quotation just because you like it, but your essay deserves better than that. Some students write from one quotation to another so that their essay becomes a collage of other people's ideas. Unfortunately, this can take no account of the different strands of *meaning* which are involved and the basis on which meaning is made (see Chapter 10 which deals with this issue in more detail). When quotations are relevant, they can trigger your thoughts and set you off along an interesting line of argument. The plundering collage artist, by contrast, has not asked why quotations are relevant or what their purpose is in building a point of view. If you are justifying your text well, you will probably create a pattern of statements, followed by supporting evidence or reasons, statements, justification, further statements, justification and so on. (You cannot leave things there, however, because you also need to take other views into account as you go along.) Commonly found sentences that lead to a quotation are:

as Wilkinson (1989: 45) pointed out,

Wilkinson (1989: 45) comments,

Alexis de Tocqueville, the early nineteenth-century political philosopher, put it rather more emphatically:

The point is supported by Wilkinson (1989: 45) when he says,

Taylor's view contrasts sharply with that of Wilkinson (1989) who says,

Comparing Wilkinson's view with that of Taylor we find he takes the following viewpoint:

This view is not accepted by Taylor, however, who is keen to point out,

As has been pointed out (Wilkinson 1989; Salisbury 1990),

It is becoming far more common to include page references along-side the author's name and the date of the reference. Years ago, if a book was quoted more than once in the same essay the terms 'op. cit.' (in the work already cited) and 'loc. cit.' (in the place/passage cited) would be used. Now we tend to use the following form for a subsequent reference in a book already cited. This has the disadvantage that you must be very thorough about keeping track of page references when you are doing your background reading.

(Wilkinson: 45–51)

(Wilkinson: 47; Salisbury: 72)

Before moving on to discuss further strategies, I want to clarify the difference between references and quotations. Both can be used to justify your writing and give it substance. References appear in the text as a signal that evidence in the form of books or papers exists and can be found elsewhere if the reader wishes to pursue this avenue. Quotations are verbatim, that is, given in the exact words of the writer, and included in the text so that readers do not have to hunt for them. The convention is to put very short, one-line references within your normal paragraph using quotation marks like this 'as if this is the actual comment made by someone else, but used in your paragraph'. Otherwise, a longer quotation appears without any quotation marks, but is indented like a verse of poetry. It is typed in single spacing even though the rest of your text is double spaced.

A reference which appears in brackets, as author and date, cannot simply be cited as evidence to support a point you make. No essay is given greater credibility because you have filled it from end to end with references. You must know exactly what the references are saying, how they differ from other views, and why you included them. A reference is generally included to turn a merely personal 'opinion' into a 'justified view'. (I will return to this point in greater detail later.)

Here are two examples of the convention of referencing. One way is to include references in the 'author-date' style of referencing as in: (Wilkinson 1989: 78). The advantage of this system is it is simple to use in the text. The disadvantage is that the reader must refer to the end of the dissertation or thesis to find the full reference. A reference can, alternatively, appear as a number listed like this (7) or like this [7] and refer to a footnote or a note at the end of a chapter. But if you use numbers, you have to make sure that the full numbered list of references at the end of a page, an essay, or chapter of an edited book coincides *exactly* with numbered references in the text. References allow readers to locate a paper or book more readily, but tend to interrupt the flow of the text. You might find that this dissuades you from using too elaborate a reference style. Bracketed references also appear in other forms such as (Buzan 1974, pp. 68–95). Whether you use a colon or a comma is often a matter of style but you must be consistent and not mix variants. Here are examples of the commonly used 'author-date' style of referencing taken from *The In-Service Training of Teachers* (1989) edited by Rob McBride. In all cases, the references would not be indented, but appear as part of normal double-spaced text.

> should perceive improvements as both 'worthwhile and possible' (Wise in Hopkins and Bollington 1988). The aims are clearly concerned with the study of a social situation with a view to improving the quality of action within it (Elliott 1982).

> Lewin who first coined the term Action Research saw it as a spiralling process involving fact-finding, planning, implementing action steps, and evaluating (see Lewin and Kemmis 1982).

> as he has pointed out in earlier works (Wilkinson 1974, 1980a, 1980b, 1985).

For books with three or more authors you can use the *et al.* convention: (Wilkinson *et al.* 1989).

Your comments, if you were comparing literature (rather than research papers), might take a form similar to the following passages from a literary essay by Richard Sheppard (1990). Notice that in the examples there is only a date within the brackets because the author's work is specifically under discussion.

> Auberon Waugh's *Path of Dallience* (1963) manages to have it both ways . . .

> And why, in *The Case of the Guilded Fly* (1944), Crispin should have made the point at length that Sir Richard . . .

As can be seen, these examples read as part of an ongoing argument or discussion. In other words, they function as part of something you are trying to say.

References are listed in full at the end of your essay and *must* have been mentioned in the text. The bibliography is a list of all the books you claim to have read (but probably have not) and this normally comes after the list of references. If you decide that a bibliography is all that is needed you can dispense with the distinction between references and bibliography. In that case, the bibliography is really a reference list, plus a few other books you have read, but not actually quoted. A true bibliography tells the reader where to find further related reading. Bibliographies and references, unless they are numbered, are always in alphabetical order. Numbered references are obviously numbered consecutively.

There are far more conventions for listing references than space permits. There is the *MHRA Style Book* (edited by Maney and Smallwood 1971) and the *MLA Handbook* (Gibaldi and Achtert 1977) among a number of others. Even though the *MLA Style Book* is sometimes called the 'Harvard system' of referencing, there are many variants preferred by higher education departments. In the social sciences and some arts subjects the following sheet is typical. I would emphasize that this is only one example and you should discover lecturers' preferences for yourself. Whatever style you use, you should be consistent about commas and full-stops in particular.

**Example of a typical style sheet for listing references at the end of your essay or dissertation**

*For books:*

Abbs, P. (1989) *A is for Aesthetic: Essays on Creative and Aesthetic Education*, London: The Falmer Press.
Adams, K.P. (1989) *Coastal Ecology*, 2nd edn (revised by P.G. Devlin and R.F. Winters), vol. 1: *The Erosion of Eastern Land Masses*, London: Allen & Unwin.
Marshall, J.D. (ed.) (1977) *The History of Lancashire County Council 1889–1974*, 2 vols, London: Martin Robertson.
Potts, R. and Wood, F. (1987) *Handbook for Sociologists*, Oxford: OUP.

*For chapters in edited books:*

Payne, R. and Pugh, D.S. (1976) 'Organizational structure and climate', in M.D. Dunnette (ed.), *Handbook of Industrial and Organizational Psychology*, Chicago: Rand McNally, pp. 1125–74.

Inclusive page numbers may be given if necessary.

*For papers and articles:*

Lewis, J. and Flynn, R. (1979) 'The implementation of urban and regional policies', *Policy and Politics* 7: 123–44.

Nicholson, R.V. and Topham, N. (1971) 'The determinants of investment in housing in local authorities: an econometric approach', *Journal of the Royal Statistical Society* A, 134: 273–320.

*For government publications and reports:*

Medical Services Review Committee (1962) *A Review of the Medical Services in Great Britain*, Porritt Report, London: HMSO.

HMSO (1974) Public Expenditure to 1977/78, Cmnd 5519, London.

*For unpublished sources:*

Paice, C. (1990) 'Hydraulic control of river bank erosion: an environmental approach', unpublished diss., University of East Anglia.

*For a chapter in a work already cited in full elsewhere in the reference list or bibliography:*

Pahl, R.E. (1971) 'Poverty and the urban system', in Chisholm and Manners (1971), pp. 126–54.

*For notes:*

If you use notes they will appear in strict order. (The term 'ibid.' can refer only to the work cited immediately before it.)

1 Quoted in M.T. Sprout, 'Mahan, evangelist of sea power', in E. M. Earle (ed.), *Makers of Modern Strategy*, Princeton, NJ: Princeton UP, 1943, pp. 442–3.
2 See Sir Halford Mackinder, *Democratic Ideals and Reality*, London: Constable, 1919, p. 194.
3 Ibid., p. 195.

## STRATEGIES LEAD TO STRUCTURE

If you have made use of the previous chapters, you will have read about several strategies for thinking and questioning. Setting up comparisons, questioning propositions, checking an argument for validity (Chapter 4) are all relevant to essay writing. Here are some conventional strategies. Ultimately, you will need to devise one which you feel you can comfortably use.

### Strategy one

1 Introduction (raise an issue?). Say why X, Y and Z are important. Say what the essay discusses and the order in which it is structured.
2 Set the context, generate a background, and touch on issues. Review the background literature if it is relevant.
3 Make specific comparisons. Give examples.
4 Construct an argument based on evidence (main body of the essay).
5 Draw some conclusions if you can. Summarize if necessary and point out any important implications.
6 Add references, bibliography and an appendix if necessary.

### Strategy two

1 Decide on approximately ten areas you want to write about.
2 Write a 'ghost' outline and introduction.
3 Write logically from paragraph to paragraph.
4 Search for a more appropriate structure.
5 Try out at least 3 structures.
6 Choose one of these and redraft the essay.
7 Look at the overall shape. Is there an argument?
8 Use a check list devised by you to see if you have considered everything you needed to consider.
9 Add references, bibliography and an appendix if needed.

## FOUR ESSENTIAL MODES OF WRITING

As any of your lecturers will tell you, there are many ways to write about the same material. Sometimes you are clarifying a point, sometimes analysing the implications of the point you just made. From the many ways in which to write, I have chosen four, each of which can act as a means of clarifying or explaining.

1 Describing
2 Interpreting
3 Generalizing
4 Hypothesizing

The commonest form of writing, and often the least understood, is *describing*. You will find that many of your lecturers despise this way of writing because it can so easily become dead and meaningless. I have heard description called the lowest possible form of writing and found it to elicit comments on essays similar to these written by lecturers.

This is just one long description with no analysis, interpretation or argument attached. What is the point of describing issues when you should really be discussing them?

Your description of life in medieval England is detailed, but so what? Unless something emerges as more important than anything else, we are left to do our own interpretation. What does it all mean? Is what you describe self-evident? Surely you want to establish a point of view?

Description may be essential if you are about to follow it with rigorous analysis and insightful comment. Rarely is it possible to sustain lengthy description without moving to other forms of writing, especially if it is passive, factual description of events and situations. If you are not sure whether your writing is descriptive without being analytical, try to find propositions within the text. If none exists, then you probably have description rather than a point of view. Description acts as a symbol from which the reader can easily understand the message or else it illustrates a point you are trying to make. If it is a symbol, then it is likely to be a powerful anecdote, verse, allegory or piece of prose which appropriately fits the context for which it is written. An anecdote rarely provides the reader with self-evidently important material and is usually supported by evidence, reflection and analysis of its meaning. If you want to use description and allow it to make its own point, you will need to give extremely good reasons for doing so.

If you are able to link description with argument, it functions in a similar way to a quotation and the reader expects you to discuss it or relate it to its context. You might, for example, describe two points of law or two kings of England and then go on to make a comparison. You might describe a social problem or a scientific discovery before going further and discussing the implications. If you did that, you would already be using the second, more analytical form of writing: interpreting.

When you are *interpreting*, it follows that there must be something to interpret. You might be looking at data you collected, description you gave, or the implementation of a principle you established. You would then be interpreting to make a point, construct an argument, or analyse what you just described. For example, you might be interpreting two views:

> We can see from the example given by Page and Tanner that their view of the experiment is remarkably different from Watson's earlier description. The main differences arise because . . .

You would then go on to analyse the pros and cons of what you were interpreting. Like most interpretations, there is probably an element of doubt about your findings. Words such as 'seems', 'indicates' and 'appears' are useful in place of words that are absolutes such as 'all', 'every', and 'proves'. (Further discussion of analysis and argument appears in Chapter 9.)

*Generalizing* as a form of writing might seem at odds with all I have said about the need to be specific in your study. There is legitimate and illegitimate generalization. You generalize legitimately when you try to draw conclusions from the evidence that you have set before the reader. Generalizing is 'seeing wider implications' and, after setting out the evidence, saying things like 'Since research demonstrates that the effect is similar to the way cells behave in rats and monkeys, then in this instance cell growth is determined by similar principles.' If you generalize in an illegitimate way, you make sweeping statements for which there is little or no basis (see Chapter 4).

*Hypothesizing* means that you attempt to look at possible implications, especially where research findings are involved or there are matters of policy or principle discussed. Hypothesizing is conjecturing, inferring or postulating on the whys and wherefores of what you have written. You write things like: 'Could it be true?', 'What happens if . . .?' and 'What are the applications?' Of course, not every essay lends itself to hypothesizing and you may not need to speculate or set up theories of the 'What if?' kind. Hypothesizing is particularly relevant if you have used a structure such as past, present and future. Since none of us knows the future, we can only speculate and hypothesize on the basis of past and present.

## FINDING AN APPROPRIATE ESSAY STYLE

The features of a good academic essay style lie somewhere between that of a seaside postcard and the voice of God. The best style is going to emerge from communicating directly and justifying your points with evidence and reasons. If you want to find models to give you some idea, an academic paper is generally more appropriate as a source than a book. Books vary much more widely and are written partly to interest the reader. They are different from essay style in several ways. When you write an essay, you are not trying to address a particularly wide audience. Unless a book is a collection of edited papers, it will probably keep the use of references and brackets to a necessary minimum so as not to interrupt the flow of text. The author has a certain right to speak from experience and make you think. A book can be functional as well as informative. It can teach as well as argue a case. Authors will often address the reader as 'you' and include material with which you might identify. This chapter is not a good model for an essay because it explains, rather than argues a case. It does not establish a history or context and there are few propositions discussed.

I will deal with some of these points. The most important feature of an essay (in the view of most lecturers I interviewed) is that it includes justification for the statements made. Justifying what you say means giving good reasons or evidence for statements and conclusions. A convention I have yet to see spelled out, but one that is nevertheless true for many essays, is that more references come in the first six pages of your essay than in the rest of the text. These consequently influence the style of what follows. If, as I mentioned earlier, you are trying to establish the intellectual level of your essay, your evidence (including references) needs to come sufficiently early. The convention may be outdated, it may be playing safe, but it still pervades a great deal of academic writing. Here, for example, is the first paragraph of this chapter rewritten using justification more appropriate to the style of an essay.

Model essays, where the structure is predetermined, are not favoured as a way to improve essay writing (Rowntree 1988; Marshall and Rowland 1983). Students all work in different ways and have different conceptions of essay writing (see Marton *et al.*, 1984: 103–23). This is hardly surprising when we consider the difference in subject content between Law, Science and the humanities. The constraints imposed by a fixed essay structure are not unlike those of a questionnaire where some questions do not allow for varied answers. As Hounsell (ibid.) pointed out, students have at least three conceptions of essays.

An essay that continued in this way would be rather dull unless you were to raise some fairly striking points. No reader wants you to continue making references for absolutely every statement made. Referring to other writers' works is not very exciting unless you can analyse and interpret what you have discovered. The references used do not appear just as extra baggage to add substance. There are already points of view being established, and the references add support.

Using 'we' instead of 'you' and 'I' in essays is also a convention that may be used if you are not confident enough to refer to yourself or your reader directly. This is not without its problems. Some lecturers do not like students using 'we' in their written work because it sounds pompous and pretentious. The use of 'we' can quickly veer towards the royal 'We' as in 'We have not found this in our data' when the author is the only person collecting and analysing data. 'I did not find this in my data' is more accurate if you refer to yourself. Better still might be something like 'The data did not show that . . .', a form which distances the reader from personal involvement. The use of 'we' is correct for a co-authored paper; or a writer might genuinely mean 'we' in respect of a group of people. For example, 'we' might be synonymous with 'the law', 'the medical profession' or 'the general public'. Alternatively, the writer may have decided to view the reader as a participant, sharing the content of the essay or book. So long as personal pronouns are used accurately they work well:

We cannot be sure what bias is brought to these situations.

We are now in a position to construct a rough model . . .

. . . though we cannot be certain of outcomes.

We will examine the reasons for this later.

I believe that another reason for . . .

I rejected this method in favour of . . .

. . . though I did not find this was confirmed.

The use of 'you' can be ambiguous and difficult for a reader to understand where it stands in place of 'one', 'all of us', or 'everyone'. If the reader is addressed directly, then 'you' is appropriate, but the style will run into difficulties where a phrase such as 'You might be forgiven for thinking . . .' is used instead of 'We might be forgiven for . . .', or 'The general public might be forgiven for . . .'. While 'you' might be the reader, it could be that the writer means 'readers in general'. How are we to know? In any case, it is worth remembering that your reader might not want to be addressed so directly in an essay. In your own mind you might be writing for a particular lecturer, but the chances are that other lecturers will also see your essay. When students use 'you' and 'your' they often mean 'everyone', or 'our'.

The over-use of personal pronouns can be very irritating. But their occasional use helps the reader identify with the writer and understand what is happening. Using 'we' occasionally is exemplified in the paragraph just quoted, beginning 'Model essays, where the structure'. Over-using 'I' or 'we' can make the text read like a confession rather than an essay, especially where these pronouns are used to start sentences. (You may be familiar with this problem if you have tried to write a letter of application giving confessional details of your own background.) The key to this is to be consistent in the use of 'I', 'you' and 'we', keeping them to a minimum. Admittedly, trying to hit the right style is extremely difficult because of readers' preferences and it is impossible to find a style to suit everyone. Many writers avoid the problem entirely by using alternative phrases such as:

Clearly this was far less true of Germany than . . .

This is where the disagreements and controversies begin . . .

The data indicates that . . .

This is not a view shared by everyone; Hounsell, for example, claims that . . .

. . . very few people would claim . . .

It is worthwhile at this stage to consider . . .

Of course, more concrete evidence is needed before . . .

Several possibilities emerge . . .

A common solution is . . .

Shortened forms such as 'isn't', 'we're', 'I'm', 'don't' and 'it's' are far too colloquial for an essay. Reserve them for letters to friends. Equally, exclamation marks are out of place in an essay that tries to make a case through reasoned argument. I would not go so far as to suggest that they should never be used, but they tend to be associated with the emphasis you might use in an informal letter. A more formal style is not improved, however, by using sub-headings and numbered lists every three paragraphs or so. If you use a sub-heading it must make the text more accessible, not turn it into a directory of short paragraphs with no coherent flow of ideas. If your essay is coherent, with one part relating to another, building to a conclusion, then you will not need many sub-headings.

There is really no point in trying to write in a self-consciously academic style as though you were dressed in the academic robes of a formal degree ceremony. A pretentious pseudo-academic style is one where you use words like 'commencing' instead of 'starting', and long-winded phrases like 'the work methods having been decided'. A further example of the 'posh writing' style is a slightly poetic one (with perhaps a hint of St Thomas Aquinas). 'Come, let us look at the health of the nation' or 'Come, let us examine the data' is a poetic plea to your reader that may go unappreciated. Unless you already use an exotic vocabulary in everyday speech, your writing may border on the ridiculous if you try it in essays. If you have the confidence to write in glorious tones, well and good. Most students are ill-advised to try it.

Style is also determined by two further factors which are the length of your sentences and the way you construct paragraphs. If you are in the habit of using long clauses to start a sentence such as 'Although we can see that the present state of research on this topic is inconclusive and controversial, more recent evidence . . .', it may be hard going trying to read your essay (see Chapter 5). I admit a bias here, since long sentences, with additional phrases, broken by commas, are not my favourite style. Sentences should vary in length just as they do in speech. There are no hard and fast rules about paragraphs, except that it is difficult to believe that there is any such thing as an 'A4' length paragraph without any breaks. If you find that you are writing a whole page of continuous text, you are certainly not expressing yourself well. A paragraph is a number of sentences on one theme and should not contain confusing jumps of thought, changes of direction and *non sequiturs.*

There are also various devices that you might use to link together parts of your essay. Words such as 'conversely', 'by contrast', 'alternatively' and 'correspondingly', can be used to begin sentences, but I feel bound to warn against the use of 'thus' and 'therefore'. If you use these words, make sure they are not used to connect together ideas which actually have no connection. (Further reading concerning style can be found in *The Elements of Style* by William Strunk and E.B. White, 1972.)

## EDITING YOUR ESSAY

The first draft of your essay is likely to be in need of editing, especially if you have let your ideas flow from paragraph to paragraph. Here is your real opportunity to give your essay shape and emphasis. You will have little idea of the final shape of the whole unless you read through the draft intending to change it. Giving your writing shape is often a matter of emphasizing one part or one argument more than others. You will need to push some parts of your essay into the background and pull others forward, as I mentioned in Chapter 3. Not every essay lends itself to this treatment, but essays that have no impact are usually those which most resemble a list of points. In essays that lack shape, the writer moves from section to section giving equal emphasis to each part so that the impression given is that the essay could go on for ever. The essay is 'sold by the metre' like a length of cloth and could be cut shorter at any point without detriment. Your essays are more likely to need a conclusion, based on what has unfolded before. A personal check list of questions for editing might look something like this.

- Does description form part of a discussion or analysis?
- Are quotations linked with comment?
- What is the main point? (Try writing it in two sentences.)
- What evidence do you use to substantiate your viewpoint?
- Is there adequate justification for statements?
- Can some issues be pulled into the foreground?
- Is there sufficient interpretation/analysis?
- Is the choice of material biased?
- Do paragraphs deal with one main idea?
- Do they link together?
- Are they relevant to the title?
- Do the points made lead to a logical conclusion?

- Are there technical errors such as grammar, spelling and punctuation?

Editing is not always a matter of erasing text. You are just as likely to add explanation and justification to give your essay emphasis. You will also be checking to see how relevant your material is; the most important editing task is likely to be to apply something similar to a 'DNA genetic test'. Imagine each paragraph carries its own genetic material derived from the essay title. It is not that every paragraph contains actual words from your title, but when you edit you need to keep it in mind and check each paragraph against your title. Not every paragraph will exactly refer to your title, but you need to avoid unwittingly changing the meaning of your title by writing about something else. For example, an essay that discusses 'Should X, Y and Z?' can easily shift to asking 'Why should X, Y and Z?' The shift is subtle, but could become a disaster.

**CHECK LIST SUMMARY**

- An arbitrary 'ghost' structure or outline can initially help you to organize and communicate your thoughts.
- You write essays because they teach you something, not just as an exercise to prove you can write.
- Writing essays clarifies your thinking and gives you some idea of how well you understand your topic.
- Turn questions into controversial propositions and question these to raise further issues.
- Irrelevant material often creeps into essays through your failure to understand what is the main issue.
- Irrelevant material can be good material that has found its way into the wrong essay or is in the wrong place.
- You cannot make your points yet ignore relevant research or literature in the field.
- When you have read potentially useful, but quite confusing material, this is when you are most likely to lose sight of your essay title.
- Plagiarism is a serious offence and far easier to detect than you might think.
- There is no such thing as a 'stand alone' quotation.
- Description rarely contains propositions.
- Generalizing is seeing wider implications.

- Hypothesizing is conjecturing, inferring or postulating.
- Check the use of 'we', 'you' and 'I'.
- A paragraph is a number of sentences on one theme.
- There is no such thing as an A4 length paragraph.
- The most important editing task is likely to be to apply your 'DNA genetic test' comparing the title with paragraphs.
- Giving your writing shape is often a matter of emphasizing one part or one argument more than any others.

## ACTION PLAN

- Plan 'ghost' outlines for an essay and choose the best.
- Construct your own check list for the editing stage of your essay.
- Ask other students their views on your essay and try to read essays by students who gained higher marks than you did. For example, what aspects did these other essays include that you did not? This might be only a matter of emphasis or specific relation of evidence to the main premise.
- Go through your draft essay and find out how many ideas it deals with.

# Chapter 7

# Making use of seminars

A virtue of the seminar system is that people get used to listening to a variety of points of view and gradually realize that other people have as much to teach them as the so-called seminar leader, who's not the fount of all wisdom and doesn't have all the answers. . . . You're not being taught; you're being provoked to learn.

(Professor of German Literature)

## ORGANIZING AND LEADING SEMINARS

Every student derives something slightly different from a seminar and the main variables in this dynamic are you, your fellow students, the number in the group, the seminar leader, the aims of the seminar, and the material under discussion. The purpose of this chapter is to point out some of the features of seminars and link them to examinations and assignment writing. First, I want to look at how students and lecturers cope with the organization of seminars.

Maddox (1988: 192–5) identifies four kinds of discussion class: group tutorials; seminars; the discussion class proper; and free or leaderless group discussion. The aims of each are different. For example, tutorial discussion groups might be organized to evaluate a student's progress, discuss an essay or help solve study difficulties. Seminars tend to be topic-oriented. The discussion class proper is usually a group of people who may appoint a chairperson and secretary and operate along formal lines. Leaderless discussion is literally that, with group leaders emerging by default and leadership changing in such a way that a group cannot be said to have a fixed or appointed leader. Maddox points out that not everyone enjoys working in a group. Some students believe that groups tend to bring into the open inequalities in the ability to express ideas. Furthermore, students who dislike one another will tend to remain silent. Rowntree (1988: 121) also adds a significant point about the way groups behave when he draws attention to the importance of listening skills, particularly as men have a tendency to interrupt women and women need to be aware of the danger of being ignored by men. A seminar is as much about group behaviour as it is about the topic under discussion.

> It takes time to involve every student, especially in a group over ten in number. You tend to set a pattern with students and they soon understand how they're expected to contribute. Within two or three weeks the pattern becomes quite hard to change, though once students feel they know each other, they're more likely to challenge one another. If you do it another way, and allow one or two confident students to argue the point, you soon have a few wallflowers on the fringe of the group . . . that's not to say the silent students get nothing from being there. It just becomes harder and harder to involve them, unless it's their turn to present a paper or lead a seminar.
>
> (Lecturer in Education)

One of the main problems for any seminar leader is whether to involve each person in turn or allow the natural cut and thrust of discussion to flow as it will. If everyone is expected to contribute, a strong group feeling of co-operation can develop. For anyone who has been part of a group that respects each other's views, discusses rather than argues, and listens rather than interrupts, the effect can be dramatic. I have known students for whom being part of a very supportive group has been a turning point in their lives. A positive co-operative group dynamic can create very strong bonds indeed between seminar members. On the other hand, allowing each group member to take turns speaking has the disadvantage that it often rules out important challenges, disagreements and critical appraisal of the seminar topic. A seminar in which each person takes turns to speak can be enjoyable without being very challenging. It will certainly lack spontaneity and a certain dynamism. The dilemma is almost impossible for lecturers to solve.

In seminars in particular, you will get a small number of students who are highly articulate, who do ask questions, who do make observations. . . . You don't want too many [articulate students] because to have too many would, unless it were a small seminar group, or a highly active one, push out the weaker ones. They would get nowhere. There's also the danger that the bright ones become the teacher's 'pets' equivalent because the teacher is looking to them, responding to them.

(Professor of Environmental Sciences)

This is not to suggest that students who observe rather than discuss are learning nothing. Some students still learn from the rest of the group even though their contribution is minimal. Groups have their own dynamics, and part of the skill of leading a group is to know when to intervene and when to let the group continue as it will. It is true to say that there are occasionally students who do not know when to stop talking. They are quite unaware of the effect they have on the rest of the group. As Groucho Marx once put it, 'If you could only wait to speak when you're spoken to, you'd never open your mouth.'

Seminar leaders make judgements about when to teach, when to intervene and when to keep quiet for the sake of the rest of the group. Some seminar members are unhappy with prolonged silences and feel they must fill them. Others are keen to dominate and have their say, regardless of anyone else. As a student, you will find it is extremely difficult to stop a particularly vocal member of a group from dominating. The onus for running groups generally falls to the seminar leader and it takes courage to change what is happening. However, if you are sufficiently irritated by imbalance within the group, or by a dominant student, there are one or two antidotes you might have the courage to try. You might feel moved to say something like: 'I'd like to hear what someone else has to say about this', or 'Can the rest of us have a little more space to contribute?' You might try to intervene by asking the seminar leader specific questions or arrange with another student to present material together. These are similar to some of the techniques which lecturers use to move the discussion on. Ultimately, imbalance within a seminar group can only be dealt with honestly and that task may again fall to the seminar leader.

Less confident students report common feelings about participating in a group. As you might guess, the larger the seminar group the more difficult it is for some students to pluck up courage to speak. Furthermore (a point not always understood by students), the longer anyone leaves it before contributing, the more difficult it is for that person to break into the group and say something. Obviously not everyone can talk at the start of a seminar, or at the same time. A seminar leader might want to involve certain students at the outset to develop a particular theme. If you are underconfident, you may find that before you quite know what has happened, other students have launched into detailed discussion. Even so, you are more likely to feel at home if you make a couple of contributions early on. This involves you and avoids pressure being brought to force a comment out of you. The key to this is to generate material before you arrive and, more importantly, generate material *as you listen*. This is often a matter of following what is said and asking yourself something like 'What would I say now if called on to speak?', 'What aspects do I agree or disagree with?' and 'How would I phrase my counter-arguments?'

The temptation to keep your response tucked away, in case you are asked for it, can actually prevent you from following the seminar. You do not hear what comes next or you lose the thread of the discussion because it does not coincide with your prepared response. Most seminars are 'of the moment', especially if the discussion is to be usefully expanded by lecturers. I believe that the chances of meeting anyone in the group who wants to destroy everything you say, and make you look a fool, are slight. Students and lecturers most likely have other reasons for wanting to hear the sound of their own voice. It is also true to say that some students are much better than others at choosing the best moment to contribute.

## POLITE DISAGREEMENT

Seminars are your introduction to the art of 'polite disagreement', a state of affairs that follows a quite recognizable pattern of social behaviour in many groups. Though groups may start by being polite, paradoxically the adjective 'polite' can be dropped from this description whenever a group has developed respect for each member. Where bonds between members are strong, there can be vicious disagreement because the members know it is not meant to be a personal attack on anyone. If you are new to seminars, it is quite usual, initially, to feel that opposition to your views, convictions and beliefs constitutes a personal attack. Most students at some stage have to go through a psychological 'pain barrier' to realize that alternative views to theirs can be just as valid. The aim of challenging anyone's views in a seminar is *to challenge the argument and not the arguer.* Those students who feel the need to attack anyone personally are probably very insecure about their position and attack because it is their best form of defence. There is, of course, a very thin line to be drawn between attacking an argument and attacking a person's beliefs.

Most likely you will feel threatened if you disagree with the majority view or have taken up a particularly rigid or extreme position. Alternatively, you might feel your views could not possibly be worth hearing because you think that everyone else in your seminar group is much more competent than you are. A solution that may help you with that problem is to prepare the seminar topic more thoroughly, so that at least you identify with the material, rather than your own difficulty in presenting it. To do that, you will need to look at views with which you disagree and try to find out why you hold the views that you do.

Rowntree describes how important it is to give feedback to the person who is talking. His claim is that you need to *let them know* that you are paying attention by reflecting back what they say, asking for points to be explained and giving all the normal eye contact and attentive body language you can – in short, to listen. While this may seem obvious, it cannot be done mechanically simply to buy yourself an opportunity to speak. When students are genuinely caught up in a discussion they give their attention to each other without having to make a special effort. Eye contact and reflection may be part of seminar technique, but the real business of seminars is to discuss ideas and learn from them.

Some lecturers have ground rules for running seminars so that participants are clear from the start about how to take part. A seminar is different from a debate in that the lecturer generally has a teaching role. This might, for instance, be to teach students about the process of arguing a case or to clarify and explain an aspect of the subject that the students are studying. The style might be to set tasks before the next seminar and expect a student, or students, to lead the discussion. Ground rules might be made clear about when to challenge and when to listen. A simple rule might be something like 'no verbal point-scoring allowed' or 'no comments to be made while a group member is speaking'. A seminar leader might explain that a ground rule is that any views that are put will automatically be greeted with the question 'Why do you think that?'

In the early stages of adjustment to seminars, lecturers will often try to teach you to stop making assumptions. This discipline is an important one. If you are unused to questioning assumptions, you may be appalled by the extent to which the whole world seems to spend most of the time making assumptions. The reality is that we make assumptions in everyday life most of the time. Otherwise day to day living would be unmanageable. Some assumptions appear as entertaining assertions or absolutes which are not meant to be taken at face value. Examples are: 'A single man in possession of a good fortune, must be in want of a wife', or 'I'm the only one around here who ever does anything', or 'Estate agents are all greedy parasites'. In academic seminars, the discipline of sharp discussion is necessary to explore topics at degree level which are conceptually more complicated. Examples might be topics within disciplines such as Physics, Philosophy or major issues such as 'democracy' and 'equal opportunities'. Unreasonable assumptions and prejudices would invalidate the evidence we might bring to argue a point of view. Lecturers may be much more rigorous about pinpointing your assumptions in a seminar or written work than they are in everyday conversation.

## A FORCE FOR CHANGE

Of the many problems that beset seminars, Satow and Evans (1983: 17) mention 'flight', and 'pairing' in particular. If a seminar group is in 'flight' the participants spend much of their time offering irrelevant anecdotes to avoid discussion. In 'pairing', a seminar group tolerates long and sometimes irrelevant interchanges between two participants. At first, the group tries to intercede, but gives up because the two who are 'pairing' take no notice of this. In cases like this, the seminar leader is a conspirator to what is happening and it may be some time before this particular pattern is recognized and changed. The onus on a seminar leader to put his or her point of view may also turn it into a monologue rather than a discussion. Discussion can also be restricted if a group thinks the aim is to guess the views which their lecturer holds. A further weakness of seminars is that, where members have no particularly strong views on a topic, they are likely to side with their friends. Despite drawbacks like these, and there are many more, if you have really taken some trouble with your preparation, participating in a seminar can boost your confidence and develop your understanding.

Seminars are a force for change and literally 'seed-sowing' of ideas. The word 'seminar' comes from the Latin *seminarium,* meaning a seed-plot – hence 'semen', a seed.

What should a student get out of a seminar? Two or three ideas. I think if a student comes away from a seminar with two or three fundamental ideas they want to chew over, then they've done pretty well. . . . You're there to sow seeds and what's important is that a question or an idea strikes home in someone's mind, because they're actively participating in that seminar, and they carry away that question or that idea and think about it. And if that's what they do, the seminar has achieved its objective.

(Professor of German Literature)

Eventually, you may be called on to lead a seminar or a discussion group. Rudduck (1983: 18) points out some of the pitfalls of chairing a discussion group. Particularly relevant is the point she makes about seminars in which the leader uses questions that limit discussion, such as 'Do we all agree?' (rather than 'What do other people think?') or 'Does anyone disagree with that?' (rather than 'Can anyone see another possible view or interpretation?').

If you are asked to lead a seminar, this gives you the opportunity to prepare more thoroughly for the rest of the group. Of course, it is quite unreasonable to suppose that students prepare thoroughly for every seminar they attend. Last-minute preparation is a way of life for many students. But as a seminar leader you have a certain right to influence the course of events by preparing well, devising your own questions and initiating the discussion. This can teach you a great deal about yourself and your ideas, especially if you pull forward issues which you think might prove useful later in examinations. You might believe that you are there to discuss your ideas with other people, but there is nothing wrong with having an eye to the future. It is very common to use a seminar to test out your own ideas. Some academics, for example, deliberately organize seminars in which students air their dissertation topics to clarify their thinking.

## HOW CAN YOU USE THE SEMINAR?

It may be that your main motive for being in seminars is to be exposed to critical teachers. Yet that is no guarantee that you will make the best use of a seminar. More likely, you will need to find your own way of deriving something useful from seminars because teaching, 'seed-sowing', and exploring ideas are so unpredictable in their outcomes. The informal nature of seminars can easily fool you into thinking that they are opportunities for cosy discussion. Additionally, this may be compounded by the fact that many students are bound to arrive at seminars bleary-eyed from the night before and ill-prepared. They will have a variety of reasons for being there. As Gibbs *et al.* (cited in Marton *et al.* 1984) conclude, many lecturers seem to be unaware of the different orientations of students towards learning and so blame them for laziness or lack of motivation. They comment:

> Most students have a complex mixture of reasons for continuing their education, and few of them aspire to (or believe themselves capable of) the pinnacle of academic achievement towards which lecturers seem to believe they should be striving.
>
> (ibid.: 187)

Given the infinitely variable motives of students, and the assorted aims of seminars, how can you derive the best learning from them? You can hardly sit there writing down everything that is said because you rule out the possibility of participating. You are hardly likely to have the self-discipline to make detailed notes on every seminar some time afterwards. However, I believe that one of the best ways to remember a seminar is to write down some of the questions which people ask *as they ask them*. This is rewarding in two ways. First, writing down a question during a session may help you to stick to the point and keep track of an issue under discussion. Second, and much more important, building a collection of seminar questions can be a good basis for revision before examinations.

Noting down questions leaves you free to participate if you want to. Some lecturers, quite sensibly, ask you to bring several questions to the seminar once you have read a paper or thought about a topic. Again, the aim is for you to arrive at a seminar having generated discussion material yourself. In some cases I found that lecturers whom I interviewed expected written work to be submitted well before the seminar was due to be held:

> Well, something I've learned from other people, and which I now follow, is that I require the written work for a seminar to be submitted *before* the discussion meeting to which it relates.

Therefore, I've got one group of people who have written essays specifically about what we will be discussing. Others will give class presentations about those subjects so that I know that a fairly high proportion of the seminar [members] will have done detailed work . . . from which they will speak.

(Professor of English and American Studies)

After a seminar, as many study skills books reiterate, reflecting on the content is an important activity if you want to develop greater understanding and improve your examination prospects. Naturally, seminars tend to finish at moments where your conversation with fellow students probably veers towards the social more than the academic and when other pressures prevent quiet reflection. Even so, if you see no relationship between one seminar and another, one idea and another, or one point you made and another, there is little hope that you did more than soak up the seminar. Without reflecting on at least the first question in the following list, you are not helping yourself to make the best of your study time.

- What was all that about?
- Where can I get more information?
- Who might I talk to?
- What are the main issues?
- Where is the most appropriate original source?
- Who has expertise?
- Does this seminar relate to other seminars and, if so, how?
- What interested me the most?
- What was confusing?

Examinations are psychologically 'in the distance'. Like visits to the dentist, they often represent inhuman activity which we would rather not contemplate. Consequently, seminars and examinations may not seem to be linked. You may have enjoyed your course, and seminars in particular, but now you discover that the examination suddenly seems to be what the degree was all about. Plenty has been written about examination anxiety and how it relates to the panic strategy of dropping all good learning intentions in favour of memorizing. In an ideal world, you would have made the rather rough notes in seminars that would prove useful to you later when revision for examinations was necessary. In practice, many notes you make are quite useless when it comes to revising for examinations. One reason is that you may have made them to keep yourself involved in lectures. Another is that there is rarely much motivation to update your notes before you begin to revise.

A compromise might be to look at your notes from time to time and imagine you have to give a fifteen-minute talk based on what you wrote. My reason for suggesting this is through my experience of marking examination scripts. Typically, examination scripts are marked under the pressure of time, especially when scripts are 'double-marked', that is, marked by two lecturers. In the case of 'double-marking', the final mark for each question is usually agreed between the two markers or goes to a third marker for arbitration or moderation. All this activity takes place within such a short space of time that the common feature of examinations is that they are written and marked extremely quickly. During examination periods, students and lecturers work against the clock. Furthermore, under test conditions, many students are likely to produce answer papers which do them far less justice than does their coursework. The reasons for this are many, but if I had to choose one examination misjudgement over any other made by students, it would be one of 'drifting from the purpose' in answering questions. So many answer papers are full of intelligent and well-informed detail which fits an entirely different examination question.

Your seminar scribbles, however slight and scrappy, will probably refer to a published paper or will sketch the sequence in which the seminar discussion took place. In my view, the most useful revision activity would be to change your scrappy notes into check lists which mapped the *sequence* in which an examination answer might be given. You do not, of course, know in advance the examination questions you will be given (though you may invent a few likely ones). The point of making sequenced check lists is that much of your degree material can be ordered in this way, so that you can call on them to fit a variety of questions. You can also do this for assignments. For example, the following sequence is typical of many good examination answers. The third part of this sequence is where the bulk of your marks is likely to be gained, so around 75 per cent of your time should be spent on putting your informed point of view:

1  the context of the question
2  nature of the problem/s it addresses
3  your (evidenced/informed) point of view

4  other relevant issues, factors
5  conclusions

You would need to change these headings so that specific seminar content could be noted. All the points that I made in Chapter 2 are relevant here. There is a world of difference between making check lists too elaborate, in the 'having' mode of study, and reminding yourself of the main issues (the 'being' mode). Seminar material can be as scrappy as you like so long as you can make good use of it. Check lists are not summaries of seminars. They become tools for the job of writing answers under timed conditions.

**CHECK LIST SUMMARY**

- A seminar is as much about group behaviour as it is about the topic that is being discussed.
- A problem for any seminar leader is whether to involve each person in turn or allow the natural cut and thrust of discussion to flow as it will.
- Generate material before you arrive and, more importantly, generate material *as you listen.*
- Challenging anyone's views in a seminar is *to challenge the argument and not the arguer.*
- In a well-run seminar, you cannot simply expect to give a personal opinion and hope for the best.
- In academic seminars, the discipline of sharp discussion is necessary to explore topics at degree level and unreasonable assumptions cannot be tolerated.
- Seminars may suffer from 'flight' and 'pairing'.
- Encourage feedback on your views.
- One of the best ways to remember a seminar is to write down some of the questions which people ask *as they ask them.*
- Reflecting on the content is an important activity if you want to develop greater understanding and improve your examination prospects.
- Provided that your personal agenda does not conflict with the seminar topic, you may be able to use discussion to feed your own ideas.
- 'Drifting from the purpose' is a problem in answering examination questions.

- The most useful revision activity would be to change your scrappy notes into check lists which mapped the *sequence* in which an examination answer might be given.

**ACTION PLAN**

- Go through any seminar notes, however scrappy, and turn them into check lists.
- Try giving a short summary of the main points of a topic to a colleague, preferably another student on the same course.
- In seminars, compare the difference between arriving at the seminar with your own agenda and just 'letting things happen'.
- Of all the seminars you attend, make sure that you experience having prepared one of them more thoroughly than any others.

# Chapter 8

# Dissertations (I): starting

Nothing decrees that a dissertation (a formal discourse) must be based on research, but in practice the majority are. Although the points made in this chapter may serve other forms of dissertation, it deals with work that includes an element of research. The broad term 'research' covers a very wide variety of activity, especially in literature and professional practice such as health and education. The intentions in this chapter are to point out some of the main features involved in preparing a dissertation and to give practical examples which you will be able to adapt to your own circumstances.

A dissertation is far more than a passive record of your research and generally involves presenting an argument or point of view. In other words, it must 'say' something and be substantiated with reasoned argument and evidence. If you want it to be interesting as well as academically convincing, you will need to raise intriguing issues and discuss them, besides presenting your outcomes. The Greek word 'thesis' means an argument and some dissertations present an argument rather in the manner of a shorter PhD thesis. Others discuss findings, results or outcomes and raise issues, but do not necessarily depend on a central original point of view as a research thesis would. In length, a dissertation will be a minimum of 8,000 words (though I have known 6,000 words described as a dissertation when data were collected and presented) and if it is a PhD thesis it could be 100,000 words long. A more usual dissertation length is between 10,000 and 40,000 words, supervised by a lecturer who monitors and helps you through the process. The point of having a supervisor is that there is no 'catch-all' way to write dissertations.

There are practical considerations. How will you choose your topic? What will you do first? What will you discuss with a supervisor? Where are your sources? Will footnotes be needed? The limitless range of topics and processes prevents there being an unassailable convention, so how might you start? Everything that was said in Chapter 6 about essay writing still applies, but starting a dissertation is obviously a much greater undertaking.

My starting point for students is to say 'What is it in six months' time, a year, or whatever the planned finishing date is, what is it you'd like to give to me, because it's something that interests you?' There's a question there that you don't know the answer to and you want to spend time answering that, so you can give me something written which, if I asked you that question, you would say 'Read my dissertation.'

(Lecturer in Economics)

Signs of curiosity, an enquiring mind and interesting questions are usually welcome traits in any student. Not everyone is naturally inquisitive, however, and some students have great difficulty finding a topic and title for their dissertation. Often this is because they unwittingly want *to write about what they already believe*. Behind a smoke-screen of enthusiasm and interest may lie beliefs and convictions destined to destroy a good dissertation. An astonishing number of students are quite unaware that they want to confirm their personal beliefs rather than discover what they do not know. A useful test to see if you are about to confirm your beliefs is to devise research questions which you want to investigate and ask yourself 'Can I be fairly certain about the answers to any of these questions?' If you are able to make a good guess what your answers will be, you have a very flimsy basis for a dissertation.

A further difficulty in deciding what to research is that for many students there seems such a wealth of topics to research that nothing immediately pushes its way into the foreground. You may experience this yourself in the early stages of choosing a topic. In addition, some students do not have strong interests in anything because they perceive everything as being complex, ambiguous and open to doubt. Consequently, they are not driven on by curiosity and may perceive writing a dissertation more as a chore than a process of personal development.

Four considerations are particularly important before starting to plan a dissertation:

- To research something you are interested in.
- To research without having fixed ideas about what the outcomes will be.
- To decide on your main purpose or question.
- To decide whether it is practical and ethical.

Clearly, you will not have much success if you pick a topic that does not interest you. Similarly, if you research something to which you already have an answer you are not researching, but *trying to make your knowledge look like research*. The third consideration is one that probably concentrates the mind more effectively than the preceding two because research is about asking questions. This is true even if the research question turns out to be 'What happens if?', 'How can we improve?', or 'Is this hypothesis confirmed or denied?' Lastly, you need a research project which takes account of practical problems such as time, equipment, ethics, and people's co-operation.

## FINDING A DISSERTATION TITLE FROM RESEARCH QUESTIONS

If your research is over a long period of time, you may find that your main research idea or purpose changes. Even so, you will need a working title and general idea of the way in which your research might proceed. You may have ten ideas, ten questions or none, but will need to decide on a main idea to ensure that data you collect will be useful. Keeping things simple in the first place means living with one focus, and one purpose to find out how you might research it. Try answering in one sentence, either of the questions 'What is my main research purpose?' or 'What is my research question?'

The research methods you choose may be very different from those in other disciplines. In some qualitative research methods it is quite usual to begin naïvely and find out what the problems are before refining the research purpose. Your working title therefore becomes very flexible indeed. The main research question may emerge from data gathered early on, rather than being in any way fixed. Researchers in this methodology gather data without pre-determining any factors. In other disciplines you may know well in advance that you are trying to confirm or deny a particular effect. In both cases, you are attempting to be rigorous. That means that you cannot let the research drift in a rudderless way.

What if you feel that nothing captures your imagination and that you cannot devise one main purpose for yourself? Where do you start if you are completely stuck for ideas?

> With some students I help a little by saying, 'Come on, there's an article. If you think of an article or book you've read which really had an impact on you and really made a point, it made a point because the writer was telling a different story from either what you knew before or a different story from what somebody else had written before, so there are questions which need to be found out.' So the way I handle that is to make them realize that there are different interpretations of things and different questions to be asked. Although you may not realize it, the article is actually answering particular questions that the author must have posed somewhere, if only subconsciously, in order to write in the first place, because it doesn't come out as something that impresses you by chance. It's because he or she was finely using tools, methods of writing, research techniques to make a point.
>
> (Lecturer in Economics)

A well-tried approach is to read two articles about a particular topic and ask why they are different and what the areas of difference might be. It also seems common sense to talk to other students, lecturers and friends so that you can begin to have a grasp of which areas may be of interest or concern to you:

> I think becoming interested in a topic is very difficult for some students, particularly for experienced professionals like teachers and managers who are proud of their skills and experience. I have heard students say that everything was fine and dandy until they began to question it, almost as if a university course was creating problems and then doing the research to solve them. They don't really want to find a topic to research because it might undermine their confidence in what they already believe. I wouldn't say they don't think their practice could be improved. It's just that they see research rather like moving the furniture around without having a good reason.
>
> (Lecturer in Education)

Discussing with fellow students and reading papers and articles will raise issues, provided that you question what you read (see Chapter 4 concerning higher order questions). A fundamental point to grasp is that ideas will hardly come to you in a flash of inspiration unless you are already immersed in reading and questioning your subject or struggling with a problem. If you are, you will be no stranger to disagreement and controversy, which are the fuel for your ideas. Whenever you read or hear about something with which you do not agree, you may be sure that somewhere there is a research topic to explore.

You may need to consider very carefully what to research before you read because the danger of reading around your subject too soon is that you may become dependent on the reading you have done. It is easy to be trapped into forming opinion too readily on the basis of your reading. (This can, of course, be avoided by doing most of your rough planning before you read.) On the other hand, you do not want to research something only to discover others have gone over the same ground many times before. Worse still, you do not want to discover that you have ignored a major piece of research just as you are about to write up your outcomes or findings. This suggests that rough planning before reading anything is a good insurance against being side-tracked. Defining your purpose can at least be attempted before you plunder the library shelves. This is not to suggest that you put off reading entirely, the reality is rather different:

> Whenever a student turns in a poor piece of work, it's almost always because they couldn't be bothered to do the background reading. Let's put it this way: I've never come across a successful student who managed to research without reading widely and thinking about what they've read.
>
> (Senior Lecturer in Education)

A good starting point may be to respond to a particular problem or source of conflict. Research is about trying to find out, provide possible solutions, test hypotheses or 'improve' things. This may seem particularly true of scientific experiment, but it also applies to researching a topic such as, 'Reducing students' anxieties in examinations'. An obvious research question in that case might be 'How can students' anxieties be reduced in examinations?' Such a question will immediately have a history to it and it would be necessary to find out what research already exists. In practice, the research already available is so extensive that we would need to ask 'What is my/your/our concern about reducing anxiety in examinations?' From there we would devise a project to find out specifically what no one else has previously researched.

Most degree work does not take the world by storm and all you are looking for is a different emphasis or a particular slant to your work. A sample of the broader research questions that are asked is given here. You will need to adapt these to suit your own subject:

- What is going on? (Surveys, evaluations, documentary)
- Is this true? (Hypothesis testing)
- What happens if? (Trial, experiment, new methodology)
- What is the solution to? (Problem-solving)
- How can I improve? (Action-research, applied research)

Whether the question or the topic comes first, there will be an underlying purpose. When you finally agree your dissertation title with your lecturer it is likely to be sharply focused, and here convention may lend a hand. Many topics are presented as an aspect of a broader field and the title is helpfully punctuated by a colon.

| | |
|---|---|
| *Purpose* | To survey and report the main difficulties experienced by a rural community in accessing social services. |
| *Title* | Access to Social Services: A Case Study of a Rural Community. |
| *Question* | How can measurement of resistance to antibiotics under laboratory conditions best be evaluated? |
| *Title* | Bacterial Resistance to Antibiotics: Evaluating Measurements made under Laboratory Conditions. |

Not all research involves hypotheses. A great deal of qualitative research involves extensive interviews where there is no intention to confirm or deny anything. The aim of the interview might be to find out people's emotional reaction to change or chart their development on a training course. I have included a hypothesis in the following example to give some idea of how one can be used:

| | |
|---|---|
| *Question* | How different is pupil self-assessment from that of the teacher and what effect does feedback have on pupils' work? |
| *Hypothesis* | When pupil self-assessment is similar to that of teachers, pupils' achievement is higher. |
| *Title* | Pupil and Teacher Assessment of Mathematics: Its Effect on Pupil Progress and Achievement in the 12–15 age range. |

A title may be sufficiently specific in its technical wording and not need a colon:

*Title*      Late Neogene Planktonic Foraminifera and Palaeoceanography of the North Atlantic.

Sometimes a question can be a specific title in itself:

*Title*      How has the Introduction of Technology affected Office Practice in the Inland Revenue?

Supervision styles vary, but a lecturer will most likely find it is easier to help you if you arrive with more than one possible working title. When you have done some of your own thinking and found at least five possible titles, the time has come to discuss them. Two common errors in devising a title are to tackle an already widely researched topic or to make your title too general. No one is going to be impressed by a title as vague as 'The Influence of Christianity on the Western Hemisphere', for example. Far better to arrive asking whether your proposed titles or subject areas are worth researching. Lecturers are there to help you refine and clarify your title, not invent it for you. Meanwhile, there is much you can do to reassure yourself that the titles you devise have some mileage in them. You can test a title to find out if it fits several research questions you know you want to ask. You can try it out on someone else who knows your subject to see if they understand it. That way at least you will arrive for a tutorial with less chance of researching in a trivial and unstructured way.

> If a student came to me and said that they wanted to write a dissertation on Kafka or Goethe I'd tell them to forget it. There's so much written they would have difficulty saying anything new. Besides that, they could easily land themselves in deep trouble with an External Examiner who knows the subject. It's as simple as that. Don't try to move into an overpopulated area of study.
>
> (Professor of German Literature)

Choosing a topic is a luxury not always on offer. For example, biochemists in one institution I contacted actually provide a list of small-scale projects that a team of lecturers is prepared to supervise. The students pick from topics and develop a personal response to prove they have researched an aspect of their course content in detail. (At PhD level, however, more freedom of choice is possible.) The following examples are broad topics and the responsibility of the student is still to sharpen the focus.

*Some broad topics offered to biochemists:*

Nervous control of atherosclerotic blood vessels
Use of enzyme inhibitors as drugs
Nineteenth-century neuroscience

The final arbiter of your title may be your supervising lecturer, Dean of Faculty, Head of Department or similar person in authority. Some institutions are very strict about approving dissertation titles and have long experience of what happens when they are lenient. The aim is to ensure that your study is worthwhile, besides being interesting to you. A particular title may interest you, but whether or not it is worth researching is quite another matter. Many institutions ask you to fill in a form to declare your dissertation title. How strict they are about sticking to this varies. One reason for agreeing a working title and sticking to it is to stop yourself continually changing your mind. Dissertations are difficult enough to write without confusing yourself further by too many shifts of direction. You may decide that, for you, a title that is fixed at the start of your planning helps to stop you wasting time.

## CHOOSING A RESEARCH METHOD

Every research method has its advantages and disadvantages, but once you have assimilated a particular style of research it is all too easy to forget the assumptions on which its rests and regard it as the main research method. There are always other ways in which to research and a variety of techniques from which to choose. Research methods are like different tools in the research tool box.

All research, it should be remembered, takes place within models, patterns or paradigms for 'truth' that are acceptable within the field you wish to research. Depending on what you believe, you will choose an appropriate tool for the research task. Essentially, each research method rests on assumptions about 'what the world is like'. T. S. Kuhn in *The Structure of Scientific Revolutions* (1970) argued that scientific research operates under assumptions which are thrown into doubt when new evidence no longer fits the existing paradigm. Science then undergoes a revolution and a new paradigm or model for truth is established to fit the growing evidence. The classic example of this paradigm shift is science's shift from Newtonian physics to Einstein's theory of relativity.

Your research is unlikely to bring about an earth-shattering shift from one paradigm to another, but much smaller shifts are still possible. These can have considerable impact for you if they change your view of 'truth'. The tool box of different methods available to you includes 'quantitative' and 'qualitative' methods. No immediate definition of these terms is going to help here because there are too many exceptions to any one definition of quantitative and qualitative. This is so despite many attempts to argue a case for or against each approach, an activity resulting in the publication of claim and counter-claim in academic journals. A thumbnail sketch can give some of the common features.

Quantitative methods tend to be associated with measuring, whereas qualitative methods deal with immeasurable features of research. Quantitative research usually measures large samples of items or people and it is not so common to focus on individuals. The focus of quantitative research is more often a comparison of extensive data measured at the beginning and end of a period of time, results being expressed as percentages, graphs or other quantifiable measurements. An example would be research into supermarket sales where a vast database of sales figures is readily available at the outset. On the basis of research over a period of time, an advertising campaign or marketing strategy might be recommended. Qualitative research generally takes smaller samples, items or groups of people and looks at the qualities in their existence. An example would be to research the process of learning to read, not simply the ability of large numbers of children before and after being exposed to a learning method. Here the research would typically result in case studies dealing with the quality of teaching and learning, and outcomes would be analysed, evaluated and reported rather than measured. Similar qualitative research is often applied to nursing and management, where the quality of a particular service is more important than quantifiable aspects.

A further feature of these two approaches concerns the style of contact made with people being researched. Do researchers try to stay on the fringe of groups they are studying and gather data by survey and questionnaire as unobtrusively as possible? Or do they gather data by becoming closely involved in the lives of those they are researching to find out what those lives mean to them?

Quantitative researchers generally try to remove themselves from involvement in any personal way with the groups of people or items being researched. They are the unobtrusive eyes of the camera or measurements of the calculator. Qualitative researchers usually have a more participant role, even living the lives of the groups they are researching. The researcher may gather information and observations through informal discussions and interviews. That way, qualitative researchers argue, people are more likely to reveal their real concerns, hopes, fears and aspirations.

It is not difficult to see that a slight change of research method or shift in point of view can fundamentally affect the nature of the research undertaken. This means that research that has already been well documented in the past can still be done if the methodology is very different. Feminist research methodology, for example, can change our perception of politics, history and education by reappraising previous research. For most of this century, history and science have been written from a male perspective which ignores gender issues. This has meant that in the Western intellectual tradition, male experience is taken as the norm and women's lived experience has been largely ignored. Feminist researchers have uncovered vast areas of history which have remained in the dark by challenging the view that man-as-the-norm is the only legitimate frame of reference or paradigm. (See Bowles and Duelli Klein 1983, for a more comprehensive view of feminist methodology.)

Following from this, one of the best ways to make use of your supervisor is to find out the advantages and disadvantages of the research methods you think you want to use. Your lecturer should act as a sounding board for your ideas and be able to steer you away from some of the pitfalls commonly experienced by students. A particularly important issue for you to discuss is your plan for gathering data. Will the methods you intend to use give you the best chance of acquiring useful data? Are there other methods you overlooked? What are the weaknesses of the data-gathering methods you have chosen? Your lecturers should be able to refer you to literature on methodology. Apart from this, you will probably need to find out how extensive your research should be in the time you have available. Such matters cannot be discovered without checking them with someone more experienced than yourself.

## FOUR CONTRASTING RESEARCH METHODS

Almost all critiques of research methods seem to be about what each method will *not* do that other methods can. Yet many criticisms are invalid where they make assumptions about the merits of one favoured research method and compare it with others. The favoured research method is taken to be the bench-mark. If we want to grasp what various research methods can offer, such value-laden words as 'unscientific', 'subjective', 'objective', 'superficial' and 'rational' are not appropriate. My reason for looking at four different research methods is to illustrate ways in which they are appropriate to different tasks. For some readers, the sketch will be all too brief; for others it may seem unnecessary. Even if you think you are already sure about the methods you want to use, it is mistaken to believe that any one favoured research style delivers unassailable 'truth'. I consider that it is essential to understand what a research method tries to do and how it goes about doing it. For more extensive explanations of different research methods see Bynner and Stribley (1979); Hammersley and Atkinson (1983); Hakim (1987); Cohen and Manion (1989); McNeill (1990); and Elliott (1991). The four contrasting methods are:

- traditional (hypothetico-deductive) research
- documentary research
- ethnographic research
- action-research

The analysis of data in all four will vary depending on whether the researcher uses a 'deductive' or 'inductive' approach. In research which is 'inductive', the researcher looks at data to see what is there, rather than gathers data to confirm or deny a hypothesis known in advance. Whatever data have been collected formulate the outcomes. The researcher might gather data, for example, in a number of searching in-depth interviews which are later transcribed from audiotape. Data are analysed to see if there is a significant picture or story emerging about people's lives. By contrast, in 'deductive' research, data are gathered in order to deduce something about, for example, a particular effect of a chemical reaction. The broad characteristics of the data are often known in advance within a trial, experiment or survey which tests or proves something. Researchers who use an 'inductive' approach are following a flexible design, looking at each slice of activity as they go along, and seeing what emerges. For the 'deductive' researcher, the question is 'What data do I need to confirm or deny this is happening?', and for the 'inductive', 'What have I got here?'

*Traditional hypothetico-deductive research* (which I have called traditional because there is no specific name to describe it) tests hypotheses, proves theories and is particularly effective where calculations and measurements are involved. It therefore tends to quantitative rather than qualitative. It also claims to be rational and objective as it usually deals with *repeatable* tests and measurements. Findings are assessed by deducing certain consequences from the hypotheses (hence the term hypothetico-deductive). This means that knowledge deduced from a hypothesis can be verified any number of times. Carr and Kemmis (1986: 63) give the following simple example:

*Hypothesis:*  All metal expands when heated.
*Deduction:*  Iron will expand when heated because it is a metal.
*Experiment:*  Find out if iron expands when heated and compare findings with the hypothesis.

The tradition stems from a school of philosophy known as 'Positivism' which says that there are laws and principles that can be applied to the world quite outside so-called subjective human judgements. The resulting view of the world is therefore that 'true' knowledge obeys scientific laws and that 'in any occurrence there is one true set of events (the facts) which is *discoverable*' (Stanley and Wise 1983, my italics). The 'Positivist' scientific tradition can be traced back to Francis Bacon in the seventeenth century and was developed by Auguste Comte in the nineteenth century (Flew 1979: 283–4). Its pedigree is a long one compared with alternative methods of research and it has the perennial attraction of being described as hard-nosed, logical and sensible.

Traditional research is sometimes misnamed 'empirical' research because of its links with Bacon and the British empiricists of the eighteenth and nineteenth centuries. In fact, all methods of research that rely on evidence from the real world rather than abstract or theoretical ideas can be called 'empirical'. Research in the natural sciences has often taken the term to mean evidence gathered in a process of experiment. Sometimes scientific researchers will go so far as to say that they believe this to be the only source of human knowledge. The term 'scientific' is often included because scientific method has the longest tradition in research of this kind.

There are many variations possible within traditional, hypothetico-deductive research, and examples can give only a snapshot of the method. Traditional researchers may set up 'before' and 'after' situations where an experimental study of matched groups of people or items is given different treatments and results are then compared. Medical trials of the effectiveness of drugs are sometimes like this. The general course of this method is for researchers to begin by selecting a topic or a problem and then to look at existing studies and any relevant theories. They then formulate a hypothesis such as 'This method of improving memory is better than that method' or 'This dosage of drug is more effective than that dosage' and design an experiment or trial to test it out. Researchers often need a matched 'control group' against which to check their findings to reduce the chances of bias within the experiment. They gather data on the effectiveness of the project, make comparisons and draw conclusions. Evidence subsequently supports or denies the hypothesis. Finally, they speculate on the implications and next steps.

In practice, scientists try to prove a hypothesis wrong rather than right. This is an efficient research short-cut because proving a hypothesis right does not necessarily mean that it will be confirmed as right on subsequent occasions. You need only to prove a hypothesis wrong once to know that it is wrong.

The advantage of hypothetico-deductive research is that it can give a clear idea of the differences between large numbers of people or items. Differences are more readily perceived than they tend to be using a small sample. The main disadvantage for anyone working in professions such as health, social work, education or management is that they often need to know more about the quality of the process, not just the difference between before and after treatment. Good nursing, for example, cannot just be a matter of measuring a patient's health, blood pressure and so on before and after nursing. Additionally, as professional expertise and competence is not always judged by examination results or the number of hospital patients who survive surgery, the research may not have findings in a conventional sense. If the aim of the research is to shed light on a changing process, there may be no point in setting up an experiment to measure findings afterwards, if the same situation can never be repeated. We are more likely to need to know how professional expertise is improved and how skills are developed *as the situation changes.*

Some researchers would say that there is no such thing as two equally matched groups of people, and research of a traditional type is highly problematic when it involves people. (A flourishing critique of the inadequacies of Positivism pervades social science where researchers reject the view that empirical scientists can become experts in investigating other people's lives.) There are further problems such as trying to make generalizations based on research that might have depended just as much on the circumstances, time and place as they did on the method used. Science also recognizes that 'facts' have limited acceptance and can never be exact, 'impartial' evidence.

*Documentary research*, in complete contrast to scientific method, does not set up experiments or trials. A student of History, for example, might spend months searching through documents to discover a fresh point of view on old sources. They might see what aspects of these documents previous researchers had overlooked, ignored or interpreted in an inappropriate way. Research into sexist attitudes between the two world wars is an example of how old German and British newspapers and books might be analysed for evidence of gender bias and attitudes. Naturally, certain degree subjects make more use of documentary evidences than others, particularly where the past is more relevant than the future. There is a documentary research methodology in literary studies known as 'reception theory' where, for example, the researcher in German Literature might look at newspaper cuttings of 1914 to see how critics received a particular play or novel when it was first performed or published. Given that there were over a hundred different newspapers published in Berlin in 1914, there are considerable sources of data on which to draw.

Documentary research has its particular disadvantages, the main one being for some researchers that it amasses many facts without any theory or conceptual framework within which to organize them. The documentary researcher has to develop a theory and try to prove it, or a hypothesis and try to confirm or deny it. It can also be argued that research documents cannot be combed for useful information until the researcher has first asked a sufficiently interesting question to know what documents to examine and from what perspective to read them. Further disadvantages are that many documents may be missing, thus giving an incomplete picture. In most cases, it is impractical for historians to interview people, either because their memory may be unreliable or because they are dead. Research of this kind also raises questions of reliability, validity and purpose. However, as all research wrestles with these questions, documentary research is in good company. For historians, documentary research can be more illuminating than using sources that are 'received opinions' from other historians. The good documentary researcher is sceptical of what other researchers have interpreted from the available evidence.

*Ethnographic research* looks at peoples' lives by participating and living the lifestyle of those groups being researched. The researcher usually attempts to become immersed in the culture of the group and makes comparisons with other groups. A major pioneer of this in the 1930s was Margaret Mead, who studied three tribes in New Guinea and found they had different attitudes to gender and adolescence (Mead 1935). Like other ethnographers, Mead gained insights into cultural differences by observing and participating with groups. Data gathered by 'participant observation' has the advantage that the researcher can draw on personal experience of another's lifestyle. By living closely with a group of people, it is possible to understand their thoughts and aspirations much better than by being an 'anonymous' observer. Set against this is the disadvantage that data can never be gathered in the same way twice. Consequently, it is not always possible to verify outcomes by repeating the research as might be the case in scientific tradition. Furthermore, the ethnographic researcher may become so involved in the study that the original research perspective is lost and poor quality data result.

*Action-research* has enjoyed an explosion of interest in professions such as education, social work, health and management. Action-research might be defined as 'the study of a social situation with a view to improving the quality of action within it' (Elliott 1991: 69). *The outcomes of action-research are generally increased knowledge, understanding and improved practice.* Action-researchers generally agree that it is a holistic approach to research, often dealing with people's personal biographies. Its attraction is that it not only finds out a great deal about professional practice, but it can also change people, policies and institutions for the better. An example of this would be where a teacher wants to improve children's ability to work in small groups and so sets up an 'action plan' to encourage them to question each other, analyse their own progress, share materials and co-operate. Evidence is gathered as the action plan is put into effect and, based on analysis of this, a further revised action-plan is formulated. If there is no 'action' to monitor, it is not action-research. If it is not systematic and interpreted as evidence, it is not even research. Action-researchers therefore gather evidence by various means such as audio-tape, field-notes, diaries, video-recording and interviews in order to find out about what is happening.

As with other research methods, there is great diversity of design and methodology. Researchers often start by gathering data from observation to ensure that they understand the context of the research as fully as possible. They particularly emphasize the need to know about the setting before they can clearly define problems and begin to find ways to improve matters.

Action-research is closer to ethnographic research than scientific experiment in that the researcher cannot stay on the fringe as an observer, but must become closely involved with the participants. The researcher is not always someone from outside coming in to research. An action-researcher will often be the person working within their own practice. A teacher, for example, might gather data about the way he or she teaches mathematics, and work closely with a researcher to analyse data and reformulate research plans. If a researcher comes in from outside the work-place there will often be such a collaborative style of data gathering that, in effect, they are co-researchers.

One of the reasons why for many people action-research can appear to be very different from traditional scientific method is that, to someone from a scientific tradition, it can appear naïve. Action-researchers often deliberately begin naïvely, not knowing the direction in which their research will go. Each stage of the research depends on what emerges from the previous stage as change is observed and recorded as data. The researcher usually produces a written case study interpreted from data collected over a period of time. A researcher who is wedded to 'Positivist' assumptions is likely to see action-research as anecdotal, biased and resulting in unrepeatable outcomes. Defenders of action-research say, however, that the assumptions of scientific method simply cannot be applied. The tendency for people and circumstances to change means that action-research is highly effective where scientific method fails.

Both ethnographic and action-research tend to generate 'rich description' which tells a story. Whatever the style, a significant feature is that whole sections of interview transcript and observation can be quoted as evidence within the main text. This is in order to allow the reader to interpret some of the data and to present outcomes as a first-hand record rather than as reported speech. The credibility of the research undertaken is vested in the *significance* of the narrative. For some researchers, the actual analysis of outcomes is viewed as interfering with the flow of the story and the thesis will be presented as continuous narrative. For others, the story is not enough and an analytical commentary must intersperse passages of narrative.

## PRACTICAL CONSIDERATIONS WHEN STARTING

It is important to understand the limitations of the methods you choose and to know how appropriate they are. It is foolish to attempt 'quantitative' research with, for example, a sample of twelve people of whom you ask three questions. A *minimum* number of people to sample would be 60 and far more than this is common. Similarly, it is a waste of time to examine a scientific process for its quality if all that matters are large-scale measurements taken before and after an experiment.

When you have finalized your working title and thought about a possible method, you are ready to discuss your half-formulated research ideas. Explaining to someone else what you are intending to do is not only necessary to clarify your mind, but gives you the chance to test the strength of your ideas on other people. Eventually, someone is likely to point out aspects you never thought of yourself. Even if this sends you into a temporary decline (as you feel thrust back to square one), it is bound to be helpful in the long run. Time taken at the start of a research project is well spent. The following are practical questions which you might ask about your research. They can only give a flavour of research style and, if you use statistics, you will need to modify these considerably:

- What data will my research method generate?
- Are these the data I really want/need?
- Am I likely to get co-operation from interviewees?
- Have I considered the possible ethics of my research?
- Where is the relevant literature held?
- What do I specifically need to check with my lecturer?
- How will I gather data?
- How will I store my data?

- Have I allowed enough time to analyse my data?
- Have I begun to list possible questions to analyse my data?
- How might I validate evidence?

Most practical of all are two short check lists. One of these is a personal check list of the possible *sequence* of your research. The other is a 'ghost' outline of the *structure* of your written dissertation. The latter we can leave aside for the present as it is the subject of the next chapter. The former will look something like this, give or take such variations as pilot studies and scientific trials. (More elaborate research may establish intermediate stages like base-lines, phases and specific steps in the research activity.)

*Possible sequence*

Choose a topic that interests you.
Read, discuss the topic.
Identify some primary and secondary sources.
Try several working titles.
Formulate your main research question or purpose.
Finalize the working title.
Examine the ethics of your research.
Discuss with a lecturer.
Finalize some decisions about the research methodology.
Organize practical equipment such as video, audio.
Make appointments to interview (if appropriate).
Set up the project.
Gather the data.
Analyse the data (in some cases as you go along).
Construct a 'ghost' structure for writing up.
Write (word-process) the draft.
Edit.
Check with a critical friend/colleague/supervisor.
Write further drafts and edit them.
Print the final copy (double spaced).
Submit bound copies on time.

Concerning the ethics of your research, you may need to sort out your position regarding confidentiality. You may also need to decide early on whether there are ethical reasons why you cannot research your chosen topic. If you are working on research involving people, you will not want to embarrass your interviewees by revealing the interview content (your discussion may later become a public document). Moreover, you cannot ethically interview people under one pretext and publish your research under another, unless you obtain the agreement of participants. Some research into psychology deliberately does this, but I take the view that people have a right to know what is going on. For example, it would not be ethical to interview people about their deepest social prejudices and then publish these as evidence in support of a party political campaign. Similarly, it is not ethical to test a new drug on patients and tell them it is an established safe treatment for their illness.

## PRACTICAL POINTS ABOUT DATA-GATHERING AND SECONDARY SOURCES

The most practical piece of advice that has emerged from discussing data-gathering with students and lecturers is:

* Avoid making hard and fast judgements until all your data have been collected and analysed.

Making value-judgements takes two particular forms, the first of which involves contaminating data collection by asking someone a question which implies a criticism or supplies an answer. Examples would be to ask 'This is a failure isn't it?' or 'You wouldn't ever do that would you?' The interviewee is conditioned to respond in a somewhat closed and predictable way, especially if the interviewer's critical tone of voice adds to the implied judgement. Certainly, the questions are not such open ones as 'How did that happen?' or 'Will you explain that in more detail?' The second form of value-judgement is even more serious. Students make various judgements about what is happening and record these as if they were actually data. Examples of value-judgements are recording such things as 'The patients were well cared for', rather than gathering extensive data about *how* the patients were cared for; writing 'This was not a good example of professional practice', rather than documenting evidence of *how* professionals work; claiming 'The target group made a success of the task', instead of recording data about *how* the group tackled the task and what outcomes were discovered.

In practice, we sometimes have to make provisional judgements to arrive at further worthwhile research questions. The fault lies in making judgements and documenting them *as if they were data*.

Simple though this advice seems, it is alarming how many students make value-judgements and regard these as data. Resist the temptation to make value-judgements without defining your criteria for judging, or you will probably bring your data collection to a grinding halt.

How we gather data depends on our assumptions about the validity of data-gathering methods. My preference when interviewing, for example, is to have some questions that I know I want to ask of every interviewee. Yet a criticism of this is that it conditions the data by creating attitudes. The following example throws into question the notion of 'truth' and the validity of data gathered by other methods:

> There is a certain set of topics you know you're interested in. The last thing you want to do is ask about them because you can immediately be accused of planting them in the other person's mind. If you wait for them to talk about the things that interest people in their job you can ask questions and arrive at a number of topics. . . . So, for example, we interviewed people who I had no idea about. They were accountants . . . engineers . . . so you have to ask them about their job before you know what issues are relevant to them. The questioning technique is to start wide and refocus in to narrow questions. Always ask for specific examples of what they say . . . 'Why is it like that? Can you give me an example?' You want people to tell stories about what they've been doing. It's through those examples that you actually know what they mean.
>
> (Action-researcher)

As the researcher explains, we bring our personal values to our research. Methods of data collection are so varied that we need to regard research findings and outcomes with the utmost caution (as many researchers have discovered to their cost). Given the opportunities for error in research design, we have good reason to be sceptical each time we hear the words 'Researchers have discovered'.

Data you gather are primary sources of evidence. There are also secondary sources of evidence and rhetoric available through reading papers and books. A practical problem is that in a certain enthusiasm to read widely, you will neglect to keep a record of the author, title, publisher and year of the paper or book. Even at the early stages of preparation keep a computerized list or a card file index. It does not take much wit to realize the benefits of wording your source of reference precisely. You will want to write the bibliography as you go along and this needs to be accurate from the first moment you copy down the details:

Thouless, R. H. and Thouless, C. R. (1990) *Straight and Crooked Thinking*, London: Hodder & Stoughton.

As I mentioned in Chapter 6, it is becoming increasingly common to give page references as well as the year of publication within the text. Keep a track of page references or you will spend hours trying to find exactly where your quotation came from. You will also find it difficult when you want to cite a work more than once (see Chapter 6, the reference to redundant terms such as 'op.cit.' and 'loc. cit.').

Many libraries have computerized databases which you can access. Most have the means to retrieve the full listing necessary for a bibliography. Through library computers, it is possible to search for papers and books not only in Britain, but in several countries. C-D ROM databases are common as are mechanisms for contacting library computers in other parts of the world. Your first call, however, is to the library staff who are generally able to point you in the direction of volumes of bibliographies. Each subject has its own bibliographies and indexes, such as the *British Education Index* and *The Science Citation Index*. There are even guides to bibliographies for some subjects, so that the task of finding what you want is more manageable. Here you will find list after list of published books and papers. Most universities and colleges operate the inter-library loan service (ILL) by means of which any book may be borrowed from another library. Photocopies of short papers may be obtained for a charge. In the UK these come through The British Library Document Supply Centre, usually within two weeks, or faster where these can be sent by electronic mail. From computer on-line databases such as ERIC (Education Resources Information Centre) a first step may be to obtain printouts of abstracts, usually about 100 words long, of the various papers you need. This can usually be done directly from C-D ROM search systems. From 200 abstracts you may find you need only a dozen or so papers in full.

These 'secondary' sources are already interpretations written by someone else. Primary sources are not yet interpreted and are, in other words, first-hand. For scientific research, a primary source is usually something within an experiment such as a change in chemical concentration or in the behaviour of a cell culture. In action-research, primary sources can be people observed directly, interview transcripts and items observed in the workplace or setting. Primary sources for documentary research are original documents such as government reports and letters. In the case of English Literature, a primary source could be a play or a novel. Apart from cultural/intellectual history, or techniques such as 'reception theory', secondary sources are critiques, commentaries, informed opinions, interpretations and findings. If you read *about* something rather than observe it for yourself, this is a secondary source.

You cannot ignore what others have done and said, but taking account of previous research raises an important question. Should you automatically believe your primary data are better and more reliable than your secondary sources? As one lecturer put it,

> If there is evidence as data or previous research we need to know what the data are evidence of. You cannot assume the data which you have collected are evidence of what you are after simply because you took the trouble to collect them. They may be evidence of something else.
>
> (Lecturer in Education)

Research methods, almost without exception, include procedures for validating evidence. This subject is mentioned again in Chapter 10, where I reinforce the point that you need to find out how your chosen research method sets about validating that *the evidence which you provide is what it seems to be.*

Apart from these practical points, it is worth remembering that data have a way of growing in quantity out of all proportion to the task. Some means of storing data is essential if you are to track down a vital piece quickly. Mark headings, leave notes attached to papers and be particular about dates and times.

## CHECK LIST SUMMARY

- Dissertation plans depend on the nature of your research.
- Some students are more concerned to write about what they believe than to research what they do not know.

## Four considerations

1  To research something you are interested in.
2  To research without knowing what the outcomes will be.
3  To decide on your main research purpose or question.
4  To decide whether it is practical.

• Paradigms for truth change as new ideas or evidence come to light and force us to reconsider our view of the world.
• Quantitative research (usually) involves measurement of large numbers of people or items researched, with little personal involvement by the researcher.
• Qualitative research (usually) involves small samples and processes, but with a high level of personal participation in observation.

## Four research methods

1  traditional research
2  documentary research
3  ethnographic research
4  action-research

• Lecturers are there to help you refine and clarify your title, not invent it for you.
• If you read about something rather than observe it for yourself this is a secondary source.
• Avoid making premature judgements as you gather data.

## ACTION PLAN

• Develop, further, more specific questions from these:

What is going on?
Is this true?
What happens if?

• Decide on your method for keeping a record of references.
• Decide how you intend to store data.
• Summarize your dissertation plans in 200 words.

# Chapter 9

# Dissertations (II): analysing and writing

> Why is it that these clever people, who may have done some nice research, approach this task with such grim foreboding?
>
> (Wason 1974 – on writing a thesis)

The answer to Wason's question may be that research is a much more sociable activity than making sense of data and writing about it. Additionally, as I pointed out in Chapter 6, reading papers, searching libraries, collecting data and discussing ideas can be confusing as well as interesting. You may think you have a clear idea of the structure of your research when you start, but weeks or months later your data can be like debris beached by a high tide. Nothing is focused, emphasized or in a form that anyone reading it would easily understand. This seems a normal stage in the process of honing ideas and constructing a reasoned argument for a dissertation. It is very common for students to go through periods of study when they feel totally confused by their ideas and downhearted about the enormity of the task they see ahead of them.

Besides this, a great deal is actually analysed by writing. Many students do their thinking as they write, rather than write down rehearsed thoughts. Lowenthal and Wason (1977: 58) identified 'holists', who think as they write, and 'serialists', whose words are already in mind, but corrected as they write. For holists, writing can be painfully slow as they work from the crudest of drafts to shape a comprehensible paragraph. Serialists may fare no better as they try continually to correct their sentences. You may not exactly fit either category, but it is still useful to try to identify which strategies help you. Chapter 3, for example, gives a summary of ideas for starting, under the heading 'Task management'.

Students report two useful writing habits concerning word-processed text. The first is to have your references file readily available on the computer as well as your text. Many word-processors allow you to switch back and forth from your main text to the references. Whenever you open brackets to make a reference, complete this by breaking off from the text and going to the reference file to enter details. If you adopt the habit of completing references at the time you use them it saves hours later on. The second habit is to keep two backup copies of your computer files, each in a different building. There are greater problems than losing your files on the computer. Theft, computer virus attacks and spilt food and drink have all been known to take their toll. Imagine arriving at your room to find an empty space where the computer used to be. Some students never leave the computer without making sure they have printed a draft copy of the last work they did.

There are two common dissertation problems concerning the writing process itself. One is that students may underestimate the feelings of isolation they are likely to experience when actually writing. Another is that they will agree a purpose for their research and then drift from that purpose without realizing they are doing so:

> I find that if a student gets into trouble that there are two very different kinds of trouble. One is that they cannot keep their mind on their purpose. They sit in a tutorial with you and agree a purpose . . . but then when they start to research they see other things going on that are just as interesting. Another serious problem is that sitting down to write is a very lonely experience and they find that they lack the discipline that sees them through the writing phase . . . so long as a student's writing something, then there's something to talk about. The really hard supervision is with a student who doesn't write anything. The student who won't write soon becomes the student who doesn't turn up [for a tutorial].

(Professor of Education)

If you embark on an extensive original piece of research, leading to a PhD, for example, do not be surprised by the loneliness of the long-distance writer. Disciplined work habits are necessary to keep track of chapters, remember what you have already written, and be able to discuss it in a viva. Some students decide that they will have to work at the writing every day to keep track of it. In a shorter dissertation, memory may serve you well. When you have drafted about 80,000 words, you may find it difficult to remember what you wrote at the beginning.

## KEEPING TO YOUR PURPOSE: ANALYSING DATA

The content which follows covers far more than you will need when writing your dissertation. The aim is to provide enough for you to chew over and adapt for your personal needs. Perfection is not possible, so you cannot expect to fulfil every demand this chapter makes. (I refer to the word data in the plural, even though it is often misused in the singular. Several quotations here use it in the singular.) Topics are:

- Analysing data
- Dissertation versus research report
- Classic dissertation structure
- Introducing your topic
- Literature use and review
- Constructing your arguments
- Coherence and justification

Data are often called 'raw data' because they are unprocessed. They can yield a wealth of information depending on the questions you ask of them, but should not be regarded as in any way perfect and impartial.

> If anyone tells you this is 'raw data' ask them who cooked it? Data has always been collected by someone, so you need to know 'What questions did they ask?' and 'Are the questions relevant to the data they collected?' It's an assumption that you can interpret 'raw data'. Surely, there's more than one interpretation of the data, so are you just picking out data to substantiate a point of view? You have to be critical of bias, selectivity and any other variables there might be.
>
> (Lecturer in Education)

Unless there are a few pegs on which to hang your data, they remain haphazard. Are you looking for certain 'facts', attitudes, behaviour or achievement? Do you want to prove a theory, explain something, compare measurements or examine the use of language? You may have good raw data, but what will your argument be? One solution is to devise categories and look for patterns in the data. Another is to browse data with an open mind and see what they suggest to you. Are there recurrent themes or results? Where are the main areas of difference? What is it that seems to conflict with a general pattern? If data are transcripts of audio-taped interviews, you may wish to highlight the transcript with comments or codes in the margin. Obviously you want to avoid being accused of bias. Interpretations of data can be biased if you:

- Interpret events as being more patterned than they are.
- Give credibility to interview content because of the importance or status of the person being interviewed.
- Leave out data because they do not fit your theory.
- Rely on one group of data to the exclusion of others.
- Fail to make clear the weaknesses of your data.

Categories for data are, after all, convenient inventions. You might have categories such as attitudes, language, and factual information. But these can distort, so you will need to make a case for why these categories are chosen. Give your reasons and criteria for choosing when you write. You need to think for yourself concerning what you believe is important. If you wait to be influenced by your supervisor, it may be much more difficult for you to write convincingly about your findings or the outcomes of your research. If you are going to write about data, you may cover areas such as:

- what you have found out
- what is important and why
- patterns and relationships that exist
- instances of agreement and conflict
- areas identified as needing further examination

In my experience students do not ask enough 'How' and 'Why' questions of their data as they write. A question such as 'Was the quality of industrial management improved?' invites a response which is meaningless, because the word 'improved' is too variable a term. Productive questions (already discussed in Chapters 3 and 4) are 'How/Why is it better than before?', 'How/Why is it different?' and 'How/Why has it improved?' At the start of your research, you go into the design of your data-collection with a number of biases and prejudices. We all take these along with us and try to be aware of as many of them as we can. You may therefore need to write about how your biases have been reconstructed by the research. Compare what you believed before you started with what you believe now.

**Qualitative data**

There are conventions in different disciplines so you need to check with your lecturer concerning the way in which qualitative data are included in your writing. The example which follows has become a conventional case study style when presenting data. It uses dialogue as it was transcribed, with explanatory brackets to help the reader. The children involved in this example have been working on a school technology project and are being interviewed by a researcher. Note that participants are not identified personally. Note how the paragraph that follows the extract is a critique of the data.

*Child R:* Well what we're doing today we had an hour in our 'launcher' [a design for a device to get a message over the security fence] . . . to get some samples and stuff like that.

*Child L:* What we do . . . you had an hour, but all you have to do is put your arm over the fence and give it enough of a push . . . but they [the teachers] did it to make it more *interesting.*

*Child R:* What we had was an hour to discuss . . . talking with our partner, to write it down on paper, see what we needed and to . . . erm do the final copy. It only took about three quarters of an hour. The fence is only about that high [indicates with hands].

*RB:* What were you going to say R?

*Child R:* The fence is only that high. You don't have to make anything.

(transcript: 17:10:91)

The above remark by Child L suggests that pupils formulated reasons why their teachers engineered tasks in the way they did. At this stage, the reason given was that it was more *interesting,* not that some aspect of learning was being promoted. I had seen pupils enthusiastically making message launchers, but when interviewed, they themselves questioned the point of the exercise. They did not at this stage refer to learning.

(Dissertation extract 1994)

This is a very brief extract and you may well need to include far more data transcription than this to ensure the reader has a chance to see how the interview progressed.

It makes sense to identify a hierarchy of issues to give your dissertation shape and direction. You may have observations concerning a rigorously tested hypothesis if one exists, or perhaps your data yield an unexpected discovery. As a dissertation writer, you will need to pull something into the foreground so that your chapters communicate ideas to a reader who has no idea what you have been doing. You are trying to find a framework you can justify as a valid interpretation.

> The way I do it myself, where students have collected a good many field notes, is to advise them to become their own theoretician as they work with their data, asking questions all the time and seeking answers to them. Even in everyday observation, not simply trying to soak up everything that's happening because that's not possible. . . . When it comes to analysing you have foregrounds and themes . . . you are trying to see if there is an inner coherence that can be forced out of the data around a particular theme.
>
> (Lecturer in Sociology)

## DISSERTATION OR REPORT?

In the case of research funded by outside bodies, the research report is a means of communication to whoever has provided the funds. For example, at one university I contacted, Economics students on their MA and PhD courses are able to charge a fee to firms for doing economic research agreed between the university, the firm and the student. This effectively means that the student writes two documents: a dissertation and a research report. The busy directors of a major firm rarely want to read a literature review and detailed discussion of academic issues in the formal style of a dissertation. They are looking for an accessible and accurate summary of the research findings, together with any important recommendations.

Sometimes the problem of having to write two documents can be solved by ensuring that the gist of the research findings can be read by turning to a dissertation summary. Further analysis is available in the main body of the study for anyone who wants to read it. The principle according to which the writing style seems to operate is one of audience: who is going to read your research report or dissertation? If it is a report, it may be tailored for a managing director and be vetted before being released for widespread public reading. Action-research dissertations, concerned with improving professional practice (for example, teaching, nursing and management), frequently adopt a more evaluative, informal style than science-based dissertations. Case studies are stories and may require you to 'tell it like it's the most exciting story you know'.

Most university departments do not consider that a research report is substantial enough to be a dissertation. You should not assume that a report is admissible. Lecturers I interviewed were suspicious of the comparative status of research reports and dissertations.

> For me, a dissertation or thesis is different from a research report because the person [dissertation writer] is learning how to do research. . . . You would expect a reflective account of the methodology employed, examining the prejudices and biases they bring to the data and interpreting it so there is a self-critique within it. Now I think you would expect that of someone who is trying to demonstrate they have developed an understanding of what it means to do research.
>
> (Professor of Education)

Distinctions between a good research report of a survey or a case study are sufficiently blurred to fuel controversy over quality and scholarship in reports. All you can do is direct your energies in a mode that is acceptable to the examining body of your institution.

## REACTIONS TO A CLASSIC DISSERTATION STRUCTURE

Dissertations and theses reveal structures, one of which many academics regard as constituting a shopping-list of essentials. It covers items any good dissertation will contain, even though actual chapter headings may disguise them. I would be surprised if your own version exactly followed this structure, but the format is common. Note particularly my comments about reviewing literature. The percentages suggested for how much to write are only a very rough guide.

**Classic structure**

*Contents*

*Abstract*    A brief synopsis of the whole dissertation (about 200–300 words).

1 *Introduction*  Includes why the study is important, its practical and theoretical significance, outlines issues and gives an overview of content. (About 10 per cent of the text.)

2 *Review of the background literature*  Critical comment on previous research literature. Sometimes this is a free-standing chapter. Other researchers slice references and critique of literature within the entire text. They take the view that the research generates the need to let a literature review permeate the writing. (About 20 per cent of the text.)

3 *Design and methodology of the research*  Includes well-argued reasons for the use of some methods rather than others. (About 10 per cent of text.)

4 *Implementation of the research*  May include any changes which occurred and relevant background. This chapter may be the first concerning the events documented as a case study. (About 15 per cent or more of text.)

5 *Presentation and analysis of data*  Results, outcomes or findings including graphs, tables or statistics where appropriate. (About 15 per cent, but more in a case study.)

6 *Comment and critique of the outcomes or findings*  A major section saying what is significant and why. (About 20 per cent or more of text.)

7 *Summary and conclusion*  Includes implications for the future; comment on limitations of the research; strengths and weaknesses. (About 10 per cent of the text.)

*References*  (which occur in the text)
*Bibliography*  (tells where else to look for further reading)
*Appendices*  (e.g. samples of questionnaires where appropriate)

One student I interviewed on an MA course said that he had spent weeks trying to find a structure within which to write about his research. In the end he had produced a structure remarkably like the classic one. Reactions from academics are also similar. They say they enjoy innovative structures devised by their students, but they also warm very positively to this classic model:

This is what I would call a fairly classic research mode. I can imagine 80 to 90 per cent of theses following something not unlike this in their presentation. And I don't think there's an awful lot wrong with it.

(Professor of Environmental Sciences)

I think this is a good outline because it is a rational reconstruction of the way research might be done. . . . What it represents is a layout which an outside reader can immediately identify with, regardless of what paradigm they are following, and read as a logical way of handling a number of topics.

(Lecturer in Economics)

Yes, there's nothing in there [the structure] that irritates me. I'd be perfectly happy with it, give or take a few minor comments. It's a good structure.

(Professor of Education)

[In the structure] I would use sections one to four to form your first chapter. The rest would form the real substance of the dissertation . . . but I think it's a good model.

(Professor of German Literature)

Some students would create separate sections for 'Design of the research' and 'Research methodology', or include additional sections such as 'Context of the research' or 'Rationale for the study'. The section that deals with how the research might have changed is usually relevant to research using pilot studies and action-research. Lecturers in literary studies are likely to adapt this structure considerably to deal with the problems of 'literary thesis'. Here, one difficulty is that students of literature are using words to research words. As one professor commented:

It [the classic structure] stops being 'literary' after a while. In literature there aren't any results of the research in the same way as there might be in a piece in psychology or whatever . . . the thesis uses the primary literature to support the argument . . . the section you've called 'Limitations of the research' probably goes at the beginning rather than the end, but you could put it at the end. [A literary thesis] . . . is innovative in that we're constantly redefining what we're trying to do.

(Professor of English and American Studies)

As you may deduce from these variations, a dissertation structure depends on the ideas you want to explore. However, there is no point reinventing the wheel by devising a structure which does a similar job but not nearly so well. Variations on the classic structure work well for most subjects because this structure sets the context of the research and takes the reader through a logically defined path. Of course, the structure rarely has such tedious titles for each chapter as are given in this example. Browsing MA/MSc dissertations and PhD theses may not reveal the true structure that underlies the writing because a good student uses more interesting chapter headings. Here are three different versions of dissertation structure. Notice that there does not appear to be a literature review, although all of these dissertations contained one.

**Example 1**

*Title:* Hydraulic Control of River Bank Erosion: An Environmental Approach

> *Contents*
> *Abstract*

1 Bank erosion and protection – an introduction
2 Experimental procedures
3 Data evaluation
4 Hydrofoils: design and appraisal
5 Summary and conclusions

> *References*
> *Bibliography*
> *Appendices*

**Example 2**

*Title:* Physiotherapy and the Disabled Child in Mainstream School

> *Contents*
> *Abstract*

1 Introduction
2 Methods
3 Subject details of survey participants
4 Case study results

5  Conclusions and recommendations

*Tables*
*Appendices*
*Bibliography*

## Example 3

*Title:* Nuclear Power, Public Acceptability and Democratic Change in South Korea

*Contents*
*Abstract*

1  Setting the scene
2  Nuclear decisions in an evolving democracy
3  The political culture of Korea
4  The Korean nuclear power programme
5  Nuclear power in a changing social environment
6  Summary and conclusions

*References*
*Bibliography*
*Appendices*

You need to decide on the weighting of each chapter because this helps to determine the substance and thoroughness of your dissertation. The longest and most substantial parts may well be the sections dealing with research outcomes, analysis and any implications of these. A dissertation which has too long an introduction or literature review suffers mainly from an overload of secondary material.

A point of style is that, particularly in scientific research, subheadings are often numbered, so that the contents page is useful for finding sections in a long and complicated dissertation. For example, using this style for numbering the chapter you are currently reading, it would look like this:

9.1  Keeping to your purpose: analysing data
9.2  Dissertation or report?
9.3  Reactions to a classic dissertation structure
9.4  A tour of the classic structure
9.5  Reviewing literature coherently
9.6  Coherence, comprehensiveness and justification

9.7   Developing your argument
9.8   Editing the text

Naturally, knowing about the classic structure does not necessarily mean you know what to put in each chapter; nor does it tell you what your argument might be. The material that follows is structured so that it covers the classic structure from sections 1 to 7. Sections 5 and 6 of the structure are often put together as data are analysed and commented on together rather than separated.

## A TOUR OF THE CLASSIC STRUCTURE

### Introduction

A variation sometimes used is to begin with a rationale for the research. The point I made in Chapter 6 still stands, that an introduction usually signals *the conceptual and intellectual level of your writing*. Introductions also provide the reader with a route map and describe the content of the dissertation. At the very least, your introduction should raise an issue, refer to research and, as far as is possible, engage the reader's attention in your main ideas. Ways of opening a chapter such as 'rocket launcher' and 'quoter' have already been rehearsed in the discussion of essays in Chapter 6; so have many basic techniques of putting material together and I will not repeat them here. Relevant topics from that chapter are: academic style, relevance and waffle, questioning propositions, making comparisons, generating a context, quoting from secondary sources, four styles of writing, and editing the text using your 'DNA genetic test'.

Your introduction should help set the context by explaining to the reader what your work is about (its purpose) and where to find its various parts (a route map). Although the introduction must come at the beginning, you may well decide to draft it much later on when you know what your introduction needs to summarize.

Four questions you might ask yourself when you write an introduction are explained here:

> I ask my students, 'Why are you bothering to write about this at all?' [the introduction] . . . I then go on to ask 'What do we already know about one part?', 'What do we already know about another part?' and 'How do these fit together?' [context setting by comparison].
>
> (Professor of Social Work)

Introductions are places where some students define their terms before outlining and reporting a case study. This is a particular problem because certain lecturers regard definitions as essential while others think they are the death of good writing. Before you become too engrossed in dissertation writing, you need to know whether or not the particular research method and general style of data gathering require you to define terms:

It [defining terms] is essential. That's part of your first or second introductory chapters. You have to get terms absolutely clear so that you can be understood. . . . I'm sure you have to define terms whatever you do. As soon as anyone starts telling me there are terms which are accepted concepts, I want to start asking why are they accepted and by whom. Where does that acceptance come from?

(Professor of German Literature)

There was a flurry of interest in defining terms in the 1930s and 1940s when it was thought that nothing had any meaning unless it was operationally defined. But it came and went because it was actually unmanageable. Nobody could ever say anything because terms can't be defined like that. Their definition is worked through by looking at the body of work as a whole. . . . I think everybody wants to be understood, but the question is how you go about being understood. . . . You've seen it in hundreds of undergraduate essays. One of the least gripping ways is to start out in an essay on 'delinquency in modern society' saying 'For the purposes of this essay by "delinquency" I mean, by "modern" I mean and by "society" I mean', by which time you've fallen asleep because everything's actually more complicated than that. . . . Things become contextually defined, but not necessarily defined at the beginning.

(Professor of Education)

Avoid dictionary definitions because they are not tailored to your specific needs. If you decide you will define terms, you may need to declare a 'working definition' to clarify matters. For example, there are numerous ways in which someone might define the term 'learning'. A working definition might be to say that learning is:

*Knowledge and understanding constructed in circumstances which allow a pupil to form a meaningful or personally significant conception from information, tasks or events encountered.*

This only goes part way because we need to know what is meant by knowledge and understanding, but it will do well enough for a working definition. 'Knowledge' for a wine taster or a surgeon is different from 'knowledge' as defined by television quiz shows testing memory. Emotionally loaded words such as 'fascist' and 'criminal' need to be carefully explained. Other suspect terms are those prone to infinite variation such as 'creativity', 'grey', 'sensible', 'sane', 'insane', 'good', 'better' and 'bad'.

Thouless and Thouless explain the difficulty of defining a term by citing the well-known example of defining the word 'beard' (1990: 36). If a man has one hair on his chin he cannot realistically be said to have a beard. We can keep adding to the number of hairs that make a beard and arrive at a figure of, say, thirty hairs at which point a man may be said to have a beard. But if we agree to that, the question is, does that mean that twenty-nine hairs do not make a beard? It is easy to ridicule the suggestion that the difference between twenty-nine and thirty hairs is the difference between having and not having a beard. A greater error that follows from this, however, is to suppose there is no way to define a continuously variable term such as 'beard'. There is a way, by arriving at a definition through the context in which we meet it, rather than trying to define it in the abstract.

## REVIEWING LITERATURE COHERENTLY

### To slice or not to slice?

Up to almost a third of some dissertations is given over to reviewing, analysing and criticizing background literature (books, papers, articles, dissertations and research reports on similar topics). If the literature review is sliced between the text, there are usually good reasons for adopting this approach. By 'slicing' I mean that whenever necessary, you bring in your references and critique of known literature throughout the text. For example, you might find that a particular event in a case study concerned human memory or assessment. There is a great deal written about both and you may take this as an opportunity to refer and critique what is known. That way, you avoid the feeling that the literature has been read after the research was done and written as a separate chapter to add credibility. There is nothing wrong with having a separate chapter devoted to literature review, but not every lecturer appreciates this format:

I don't particularly like literature reviews at the beginning of the thesis . . . usually my experience is that the subsequent research appears to be totally unrelated to the literature review. Now that doesn't mean I'm against literature reviews, but just as a kind of conventional thing that they feel they've got to do. I read too many PhDs that have these lengthy literature reviews – say, a quarter to third of the thesis – and then the subsequent research reported after that seems to be only marginally related . . . so what I advise people to do, is to demonstrate that you can use the literature to develop your own thinking and analysis of data, and that maybe the point of referring to the literature is that it helps your own thinking about the data that you are actually analysing. So in a sense the reference to the literature should be part of your analysis [as you go along].

(Professor of Education)

If you are writing a case study, the literature and its significance is something which emerges from the case study as being necessary. If the subsequent research appears unrelated to the literature, you have the wrong kind of review. In reviews which are separate, you have a chance to debate the assumptions and inadequacies of the viewpoints you have read. But a separate chapter must function as a relevant context for your research. Superficially, a literature review demonstrates that you have done some reading and considered it. In practice you review literature to define the space that has previously been neglected by researchers. This helps determine, in a thesis, how original your contribution might be. You also establish the theoretical framework of your study. In the process of reviewing, you establish the context and significance of the field of study. An examiner will certainly be familiar with the literature, so avoid name-dropping a long list of writers and researchers for the sake. Good literature reviews are creative and analytical. Every part of your review should contribute to issues surrounding your central research concerns.

A good reason for having a separate literature review would be that you needed to ensure that your position regarding the field of research was made very clear at the outset. The remainder would then be a reflection on the position you had taken regarding the field of study. You would, of course, inevitably demonstrate that you knew the literature and were not leaving out anything important before you proceeded to the next chapter. Three short examples illustrate aspects of literature reviews. They are taken from MA dissertations with the permission of the authors.

## Comparing

Aiming to find out what parents perceived to be the purpose of education, Olneck and Bills (1980) found that the majority of low-income parents in their study had minimal expectations of schools. This had been compounded by Brantlinger's work (1985) on the expectations of low-income parents. She found that . . .

(Angela Stephenson 1988)

## Criticizing and raising issues

Kerry and Eggleston's (1988) attempts to explain the shift in terms of contextual influences, the nature of primary teachers, responses to mixed ability classes and open plan schools only begins to touch on the problem for me. If 'schools are slow to adapt and evolve' (Kerry and Eggleston 1988: 33) how was it possible for such a major shift to occur? More fundamentally, has change really happened? . . . Even Kerry and Eggleston's (1988: 16) cameos give little indication of the influence of the children.

(Shelagh MacDonald 1989)

## Relating points to those of other researchers

Relating this to Elliott and Adelman's analysis suggests that global learners would find unstructured open-ended enquiry less rewarding and would tend to maintain instability by demanding dependence on the teacher. This dichotomy represents . . .

(Ibid.)

You may find that the following starting points are useful to you in triggering changes of direction in your writing:

Previous research offers us a number of examples . . .
What can be said immediately is . . .
This clash of views calls into question . . .
It would hardly be an exaggeration to say that . . .

The problem can be summarized . . .
The problem can be seen from another angle . . .
Is this a really sound reason for saying. . ?
A second argument which cannot be ignored is . . .
We must allow for . . .
From this, it would seem that not all . . .
This explains why . . .
Alternatively, . . . in addition . . . by contrast
One of the most striking examples . . .
A similar theme is taken up by . . . who says that . . .

## The remaining chapters

Some students next go on to discuss the design of the research and its methodology. In action-research this can be slightly different because the methodology changes as the research progresses. The methodology is determined by examining outcomes at each cycle of the research activity and all that may be written is a chapter entitled 'Methodology statement'. In this you would discuss the nature of qualitative methodology and the principles you used in deciding how to gather data. In other research styles, the methodology would be tightly organized in advance. You would declare sampling methods, statistical methods, problems of questionnaire design and any limitations you could envisage.

Your dissertation is likely to cover the implementation of your research, presentation of results or outcomes, and the analysis of these. If results are to be presented, you may need to use graphs and tables. You might be tempted to anticipate findings and implications, but this really comes later. You will have ample opportunity to do this in your final chapters. Presentation of results may be a short chapter if it is simply a presentation. If it is woven into analytical comment as you go along, the final chapters will be taken as longer analysis and discussion without such an obvious break. Styles vary, but it is important to decide whether you are presenting results or combining these with analysis. Otherwise you will repeat yourself in chapters that follow. Even a style which is a narrative 'story-telling' approach needs points of insight and emphasis.

Of all sections, the chapters which discuss outcomes or findings are the most important to write well. An examiner will turn to these because the conclusions you draw signal your ability to make sense of data. In case studies involving interviews, the convention is to cite sections of transcribed audiotaped or videotaped inter-view verbatim. If you make the error of trying to narrate the evidence you write such comments as 'One of the managers felt that the communication procedures were inadequate' or 'In one worker's opinion' instead of giving the relevant transcript. If you do not cite examples directly, in the manner deemed appropriate to the discipline, then you could be accused of making it up. Narrated 'paraphrased evidence' is really still a claim waiting to be supported by genuinely cited data. In some cases, you might solve this problem by referring to data which can be found in your appendices.

A convention in numerous case studies is to have a section which says something about the reasons why you chose to interpret data the way you did. Some idea of the status or importance of specific data can help to establish a valid interpretation. You need to make a case for the interpretation you give because this is unlikely to be self-evident. You need to declare points of tension, difficulties and areas of uncertainty. In the discussion of outcomes you also need to refer back to the theoretical underpinnings of your work, which you discussed in your second chapter or in the introduction. There should be *a direct link between outcomes and the theoretical ideas* which you introduced earlier. (In the strict classic structure, you would refer back to Chapters 2 and 6.)

Whatever you decide is to be the structure for your remaining chapters, you need to avoid taking the reader back and forth using the same material in more than one chapter. Ultimately the quality of your work will be judged on the way you have related parts to the whole, yet kept a clear view of the structure. The later stages of a dissertation are a point at which you need to ask 'How does this match my starting point?' Refer back to some of the earlier ideas, or re-write your introduction to take account of later develop-ments. You want to demonstrate that you are still aware of the way in which you started and have not drifted so far that you make earlier text look irrelevant.

## COHERENCE, COMPREHENSIVENESS AND JUSTIFICATION

*Coherence* is the extent to which you are able to make one section of your dissertation relate logically to another and give it a quality of 'wholeness'. At this point you may begin to feel I have set impossible conditions for success. Remember that these are aspects of writing meant to make your work better than it was. If your work is even one sentence better, then it is better. Suppose your dissertation is an argument (thesis). This should pervade the text as a thread from start to finish. Within each chapter, coherence is the quality of 'holding together' ideas, comparisons and discussion. Nothing is left isolated, free-standing and separate from the general thrust of the writing. Look at what you have written and ask yourself 'Where is the connection with anything else?'

The whole thing 'says' something. It's going somewhere, From the first word to the last it should be building up to saying something and 'coherence' is the degree to which the whole thing makes sense. For example, a method chapter could be very clear in itself, except you forgot to tell the reader what your purpose was or why you were doing it. And therefore it's not coherent. While it's a bone fide account of what you did, your reader doesn't have a clue why you did it.

(Professor of Education)

*Comprehensiveness* is the extensiveness of literature consulted and the extent to which a wide range of data are taken into account. Your dissertation should not be broad for its own sake, but relate comprehensively to the central ideas you chose to emphasize. A dissertation which is insufficiently comprehensive ignores too much of the available literature and does not discuss alternative viewpoints. You need to avoid making your dissertation 'bitty' and fragmented by keeping an eye on coherence as well as comprehensiveness. Your objective is to make your dissertation comprehensive without destroying the thread of your argument.

I have already begun to discuss the third element, known as *justification*, in Chapter 6. There, I described the pattern of making statements followed immediately by supporting evidence or reasons, statements, justification, further statements, justification, and so on. (I also pointed out that you could not stick rigidly to that pattern because you need to take other views into account as you go along.) In a dissertation, you will not only justify your use of data, you will also have to justify the design and methods of your research so that you make a good case for saying why you rejected some methods and chose others. An examiner does not necessarily have to agree with what you say and will normally be satisfied, *provided that you make a good case*. There is no need to perceive this as negative because it can be very positive:

Sometimes it's rather like waiting to be attacked and that's the problem. You could be dragged into writing in a very defensive way . . . referencing and justifying everything until you daren't take any risks at all. It's true that you need to be cautious in what you say and justify it, but caution need not kill off a good enthusiastic piece of research. So long as your evidence is sound you need only look at what you write with a sceptical eye and support with evidence rather than defend yourself unnecessarily. Supporting and defending are quite different.

(Lecturer in Education)

## DEVELOPING YOUR ARGUMENT

If you disregard your overall strategic point of view, the dissertation makes too many demands of the reader to discover the significance of your research. Within any overall argument there will be much shorter attempts to argue specific points. One way in which you might develop an argument is deliberately to declare points of view, make propositions and substantiate them by eroding any challenge or counter-argument. This is the 'legal' model of argument, an example of which might be to choose one of two alternatives and argue a case for and against.

*Issue:*          Who pays for oil pollution?

*Proposition A:*  The oil companies should pay for pollution.
*Proposition B:*  The government should pay for pollution.

Arguing your case is rarely as simple as picking one of two propositions because a third, fourth or fifth proposition may be equally feasible. Proposition C might be: 'Both should pay', and proposition D might be: 'Neither should pay'. Even so, you may decide to *argue* for one proposition against its main contenders to give your dissertation some bite. Alternatively, you may think that none of these propositions is sound because you believe that prevention of pollution is a much greater issue than cleaning up oil slicks. In that case you would examine several competing propositions and point out their merits and weaknesses.

This is what I will call the 'television panel' model of argument, where a panel of analysts, usually four people, present their propositions and argument in response to a news item. They take up particular positions in turn and may even compete for supremacy. Transferring this model to your dissertation, you would begin by examining four or five propositions. You might argue over the consequences of accepting (or rejecting) each view. Your main argument might be: 'None of the propositions is true because . . . and these are the consequences.' Furthermore, you might wish to argue for particular recommendations based on your analysis of four or five propositions which arose from your findings or outcomes. Whether you employ the 'legal' model, 'television panel' or a variant of your own, taking a particular position is a useful way to develop a conclusive argument. This gives you a chance to expand on your writing rather than be cryptic.

In Chapter 6 I disparaged isolated examples of description in essays. Your research will, of course, need to be described and explained, but you need a very good reason why description alone is enough. In qualitative case study research there is 'rich description' of the case study. This is to bring alive the narrative, but it is still not bland description or simply the retelling of events. Description must function as more than mere scene-setting.

In subjects like Literature, a student's descriptive writing tends often to be purposeless retelling of the plot:

I say to my students 'Don't retell the plot. I know it better than you do.' You need to look at *how* the author tells you rather than *what* the author tells you. How is this making an impression on you? . . . I do a lot of comparing of text and ask 'Where else have you seen this theme come up?', 'How is this different?' . . . You do try to guide your students to keep them out of dead ends. If they choose some topic they can live with for a couple of years they will have plenty to write about . . . they have to prove to me why what they're doing is worth doing. They must engage with the text and make comparisons . . . I teach them how much to document with references and how much to leave alone. They must support their claims with logical reasons or references to back up what they say. How much of it is yours, how much general knowledge and how much needs referencing?

(Lecturer in Spanish Studies)

Readers of your work expect you to follow description with interpretation, unless the description is an interpretation in itself. Usually there is analysis and criticism. The more you describe blandly without pausing to reflect and comment, the more you build an expectation in the reader that you will analyse. Ask yourself what your description reveals to the reader.

Interpreting your descriptive passages of text is done partly by comparing similarities, differences, criticizing and discussing threads and themes. Of these, comparing and contrasting are likely to produce further pages of writing because they can sharply focus your thoughts. Rarely are there self-evident comparisons. Most need to be discovered and worked at, so that you can say something worthwhile about them. Ask yourself 'What can I find to compare?' Essentially you are constructing meaning and demonstrating the grounds on which your meaning has been made (see Chapter 10 for a further discussion of meaning).

Some students are known to put their argument the wrong way round. You do not construct a good argument by starting to describe evidence upon evidence and then saying at the end: 'Here is all the evidence so the following must therefore be true.' An argument will have a sequence. Often it begins with a context to set some limits to the possible breadth of the argument. From there it is likely to state a proposition or propositions and seek further support by a mixture of evidence, erosion of counter-argument, and provision of further evidence. It will raise issues, but maintain its initial impetus and thread. In a nutshell, an argument has a logical sequence of points leading to a conclusion or conclusions. By this means an argument becomes a valid (legal, logically correct) argument (see Chapter 4, 'Questioning the truth of a proposition', and Chapter 10 concerning validity).

When you have drafted your dissertation, it might be examined to see if arguments contain the following commonly-found errors. The list is not comprehensive, but in my view a bad argument may contain statements which:

- contradict themselves
- have no relationship with previous statements
- do not have any logical sequence
- are based on assumptions that were never questioned
- appeal to authorities that are known to be limited or suspect (e.g. dictionaries, historical traditions long discredited, research now challenged, famous people, writers of fiction or politicians whose only authority is that they are well known)
- present opinion as argument unsupported by evidence
- contain nothing that leads to a logical conclusion
- take no account of exceptions or counter-claims
- try to claim *absolute* instead of qualified truths

The above reference to absolute truths (or more correctly, absolute statements, since truth is far too complex a concept to submit to absolutes) is an important one. By the time PhD students have researched their topic, it is surprising how adept they have become at qualifying their remarks by such phrases as 'The data *suggest*' rather than 'The data *show*', *indicates*, rather than *conclusively proves*, and *possibly*, rather than *certainly*. Researchers can, of course, be accused of sitting on the fence if they qualify their claims, but the reality is that very few statements can be made without there being an element of doubt about them. This is true of qualitative research which involves people, where measurement and proof are absent from the methods used. In qualitative research, outcomes are almost always tentative unless you are doing something as lengthy as a PhD. Even then, you are justifying an interpretation which may have few generalizable features.

## EDITING THE TEXT

Apart from your dissertation supervisor, you need to find a critical friend who is prepared to scribble on your draft whenever a sentence or a paragraph is not clear. Your supervisor may do this at some stage, but in my experience you need someone else who will make a much earlier criticism of your draft. You should not, however, respond immediately to the criticisms made. Your critic may be right, but another reader could disagree, so you must weigh criticisms carefully. Clarifying a point you are making is much easier to handle than changing an idea or revising a point of view. Here, you would simply work on the passage until it made the same sense to other readers as it does to you. A mistake reported by some students is to have handed their draft to a critical friend far too early and found they needed to have it criticized a second time. A second reading of the revised draft is not always so enthusiastically undertaken, a point to be kept in mind when you hand a draft to your supervisor. If you are checking to see if propositions are supported, you are unlikely to find yourself returning to these questions:

'Is it true?', 'Is it relevant?' and 'What are the implications?' are questions that any student ought to be asking at whatever level he or she is working. Whether they're writing a four-page undergraduate essay or a 100,000-word thesis, the questions I ask most frequently are 'Why?' and 'Where's the evidence?'

(Professor of German Literature)

The question 'Is it true?' has obvious limitations, as I mentioned in the previous chapter. But it is still a useful question. Depending on your view of the meaning of 'truth', you can say there is no such thing as 'a fact' or no such thing as 'truth'. I believe you ask that question in any case, knowing there are greater and lesser degrees of truth. You ask it to find out whether some findings are more certain than others.

A final check of the writing is likely to be a matter of looking at the coherence and shape of the argument. Are there enough analogies and examples? Practical considerations are to check spelling, grammar, punctuation, and so on against a check list or the style sheet used by your institution. A particular check should be made on references to see if you have included them in the reference list and listed them accurately. These small details show you are professional about the conventions. Dissertations are usually bound and almost without exception word-processed, leaving a generous left-hand margin for binding (the cover using a form and colour approved by your institution). The time scale of this is such that at least a month should be left for final printing and binding. A minor point to add is that some students using word-processors have a habit of making their paragraphs almost the same length, as the number of lines they can see on the screen. Check for variety in paragraph length because paragraphs should vary according to the ideas contained within them.

Starting to write is perhaps best summed up in a quotation from an American book catalogue, passed on to me by a lecturer in Latin American and Spanish Studies: 'There is nothing to writing. Just sit down at a word-processor and open a vein.'

## CHECK LIST SUMMARY

- Students will agree a purpose for their research, then drift from that purpose without realizing.
- Writing is for many people a solitary experience.
- Ask 'How might I analyse my data further?'
- What issues look as if they are likely to be important?
- What issues might I have missed?
- Where do patterns emerge?
- What methods of presentation are needed? (graphs, tables)
- Categories for data are, after all, convenient inventions.

- No examiner wants to be faced with the task of guessing what you meant to say.
- An introduction can signal the conceptual and intellectual level of your writing.
- There are good and bad definitions
- In reviews of the literature you have a chance to debate the assumptions and adequacy of the viewpoints you have read.
- These may be written as a separate chapter or 'sliced' throughout the text.
- Description is usually accompanied by analysis and comment.
- Narrated, paraphrased 'evidence' is really a claim waiting to be supported by genuinely cited evidence.
- Alongside 'coherence' go 'comprehensiveness' and 'justification'.
- Checking for justification means asking yourself 'Why?' and 'Where's the evidence?'
- Whatever the quirks of institutional style in presenting your writing, you should follow them exactly to the letter. This includes preferences for binding (including colour of the cover).

## ACTION PLAN

- Find out where your institution keeps completed dissertations and look at several, making sure you discover which ones are thought to be worth browsing.
- Use a highlight pen to identify 'evidence' in your drafted text and other data.
- Find links between chapters of your work and note if they constitute 'coherence'. Search for lack of 'coherence'.
- Look at the final draft of the text to see if the introduction needs changing.
- Refer to Chapter 4 and look for questionable propositions.
- Find out your 'handing in' date, allowing a month for final printing and binding. Work backwards to devise a timetable for yourself.
- Make a check list of the mundane but essential things like checking references, spellings and double-spacing of text.

# Chapter 10

# Reliability, validity and meaning

This chapter looks at issues that are central to quality in written work, particularly at MA/MSc level and beyond. I have assumed that, like most students, you will be assessed mainly through your written work, whether this is a piece of literary criticism, dissertation, research report or essay. This is not to deny activities such as assessment by viva voce, practical examinations and seminar presentations. The view I put forward is that understanding some of the problems associated with evidence and meaning-making will help you to look again at the way you study and write. There is no way to define quality without falling into the trap of thinking it can be pinned down in a few words. The ideas that I discuss here are intended to persuade you that one of the main attractions of study is that it reveals yet deeper levels of meaning and understanding.

Lecturers who were interviewed for this book repeatedly mentioned two essentials for any good piece of academic written work. First, that a good piece of work has a thread, theme or argument. Second, that a good piece of work is justified (substantiated) throughout by sound evidence which has been critically appraised. That means it is reliable, valid and convincing evidence which supports an argument, a point of view or a conclusion. Lecturers who were asked about 'justification' (see also the examples in Chapters 6 and 9), spoke of this as one of the foundations of study in any discipline. Whether students were considering arguments or writing them themselves, argument and justification were agreed to be high on the academic agenda.

Justification is one of the two things that come top of my list. The first one is to have some clear sense of an overall strategic argument. The second is to have the factual evidence with which to justify that argument. The two things seem to me to be of equal importance.

(Professor of German Literature)

I'm looking for evidence to support whatever she or he is asserting. . . . Depending on what discipline you're in and depending on what political context you are in, certain things are accepted as evidence or not. So there isn't a unique form of knowledge or evidence that is highly disciplined and politically specific.

(Lecturer in Economics)

You can't really have evidence without an argument and you can't have an argument without evidence.

(Lecturer in Development Studies)

Well, I tend to tell them that an essay is an argument; that they must presume a reader who is not necessarily convinced of the argument that they are going to advance. They therefore have to take the reader through it step by step, convincing them by producing evidence of what they are saying . . . they can only do that by presuming a sceptical but persuadable reader. . . . 'Is it true?', 'Where's the evidence?' is what I'm saying when I ask them to develop an argument and then test it against the primary source.

(Professor of English and American Studies)

One sort of evidence is the evidence provided by the literature. The next sort of evidence is that particularly related to original research . . . some examples of transcripts [of interviews] in my appendix . . . raw data, or primary source material, will be evidence that shows that I really have collected what I say I have. Then there's evidence to support interpretation or explanation. And it seems to me that simply giving my own opinion to support an explanation isn't enough evidence. I need to use various research methods to indicate that the opinion, or the explanation, or the interpretation of data arrived at is justifiable.

(PhD Student)

This raises the question of what might constitute sound evidence to support an argument or justify a piece of research. Naturally, the different disciplines of study have their own understanding of evidence and its purpose in research. Some researchers talk of an argument being 'justified', others 'proved', and yet more refer to 'informed' evidence. Yet, regardless of the discipline, there is not much point providing evidence if it is unreliable, irrelevant or in any way invalid. The quality of your work may stand or fall by your understanding of the appropriateness of the evidence which you offer to support or deny a point of view.

## THE IMPORTANCE OF CONTEXT AND STATUS

Arguments which we put for or against partly depend for their credibility on the value or significance of the examples we provide. To know how significant evidence is, we need a very thorough grasp of the context in which it is presented. In a piece of written work, this is why you would take so much trouble to establish a context for your work at the beginning. There are, however, two further ways in which you establish 'context'. One is obviously within a paragraph so that the meaning of words is clear; the paragraph contains related ideas and becomes the context for your main points. The other is the context of your primary or secondary *sources* of evidence. A simple example would be if we cited the work of a researcher (we will call her Wilkinson) and referenced in the usual way, as in: (Wilkinson 1989). If we refer to Wilkinson, we are also referring to the context in which her work took place. In other words, we bring a whole package of questionable issues about reliability, relevance and validity of evidence with each reference we use.

Clearly, we cannot question everything forever, but arguments nevertheless depend on the relevance and significance of their supporting evidence. This is determined partly by asking questions about the reliability of its original context, partly by the appropriateness of the context in which we decide to use the evidence. Did Wilkinson use a valid research method? Were there questionnaires? If so, what percentage was returned? What were the biases in the questions asked or answers given? Most importantly, does Wilkinson's work really support or deny the point you are trying to make? Who else has produced evidence which conflicts with Wilkinson's research or arguments?

Even if you are convinced that the context of your evidence is appropriate, sound arguments depend on making the necessary connections with personal experience to understand them. Martin Hollis, in his book *Invitation to Philosophy* (1985), points out that arguments are logically sound for us, only if we understand the connections which are being suggested. If we give reasons for asserting that something is true, we cannot argue using inappropriate examples which nobody else understands. As Best (1985: 61) summarizes very clearly, there is 'a distinction between having a valid reason and having a valid reason which the other person can understand'. Hollis gives a summary of ground rules for developing a reasoned argument, of which two concerning evidence are particularly relevant here:

- Sound uses of evidence rely on drawing analogies with known cases of the same pattern.
- They are not a proof that the conclusion follows logically from the evidence: they show that the conclusion is probable on the evidence.

Hollis strikes a note of caution. As he reiterates, 'Evidence is good evidence only if there happen to be suitable connections in our experience.' If you are working within a particular discipline, you will need to find out what constitutes evidence, within your chosen field of study. It may not matter so much that evidence differs from one discipline to another, but it matters a great deal that you understand what is meant by good evidence *within your subject discipline.* Research methods, and experience of ways in which to provide evidence, cannot simply be swept aside as if nothing has happened within the discipline since the beginning of time. Quantitative researchers, qualitative researchers, scientists, ethnographers and action-researchers all have their elaborate means of ensuring that evidence contributes in particular and appropriate ways. You cannot assume a universal understanding of the term 'evidence'. Nor can you assume that evidence is significant just because you think it is. Consider, for example, the following propositions:

- Evidence can be valuable and significant, but irrelevant to your argument.
- Evidence can be relevant to your argument, but trivial or superficial.

If you were to explore these propositions, the short-hand term *status* could be very useful. Evidence has status within certain conditions which you declare in support of a point of view. The status of evidence is determined by its value, significance and relevance to the context to which it relates. The two examples above could, for example, apply to the criminal who carries with him both a sharp knife and a box of matches. The status of evidence which included these two items might be determined differently in a context of arson or one of malicious wounding. If you are going to provide evidence, it must be appraised and its status established before you cite it.

There are pressing reasons to do this. Examiners, lecturers and others bring their own values to anything that you write or discuss with them. Consequently, you are up against the particular experiences they have had and the embedded beliefs which they hold. A classic predicament for anyone who is trying to present evidence is one of being misunderstood by someone else whose beliefs and paradigms are different.

A naïve view of this problem is to think that all paradigms are relative and that the perceptions of one person are just different from those of anyone else. Our personally constructed paradigm, so the argument goes, exists in relation to everyone else's view of the world and is equally valid. We hold perceptions which are, to some extent, personally biased, political, psychological and value-laden, but so does everyone else. Unless we question them, or new evidence jolts our thinking, we can stand permanently in the shower of our own value systems. There are, however, difficulties adhering to the notion of a 'world view' or personally constructed set of perceptions. While we all inhabit a 'world view', it is not simply a matter of relativity, but of necessity. We may have very little choice about how we come to understand the world. We only develop a 'world view' at all through the public language system in which we participate. The point is that we cannot step outside this; we can examine only from within our own language system. In so far as values, assumptions, customs and beliefs are embedded in language, they are fundamental to our 'world view'. Consequently, each of us carries assumptions about how the world exists and, within a study discipline, we also carry the values that have determined that discipline. The natural scientist, for example, proceeds on the assumption that the world has some sort of order and is amenable to systematic enquiry. This is still an assumption, even if scientists have adopted systematic enquiry as their main method of understanding the world.

Standing within 'a tradition of thought', what effect does that have on the comparisons that we make? Inevitably, there is no such thing as an *impartial* comparison, a factor which has considerable implications for the claimed accuracy of research methods and academic criticism. We make comparisons as best we can, trying to be aware of our own position. I am not suggesting that every piece of written work that you produce should question the tradition in which it operates. But many assignments and dissertations need to include reasons for preferring one procedure to another, one model for academic criticism, a particular research method or evaluation of a text. My point is that it is possible to devise elaborate procedures, refer to seminal writers, and delude yourself that you are providing 'facts' or 'factual evidence'. Not even the terms 'fact' or 'factual evidence' are universally acceptable. If researchers and writers seem cautious in their claims, it is with good reason. Embedded assumptions are a form of academic blindness and it is very difficult to be aware of the limitations of your own vision.

A more positive way to look at this is to live with the limitations which are inherent in all study and see where they lead. In mathematics, for example, the term 'factual evidence' is understood within certain meanings which are agreed between mathematicians. What we make of these agreements, however, is much more important, as the mathematician and astronomer Bondi explains:

> I regard the very use of the word 'fact' as misleading, because 'fact' is an emotive word which suggests something hard and firm. What we have in science is always a jumble of observation, understanding of the equipment with which the observation was carried out, interpretation and analysis. We can never clear one from the other. Certain experiments that were interpreted in a particular way in their day we now interpret quite differently – but they might well have been claimed as 'facts' in those days. . . . It's important to realize that in science it isn't a question of who is right and who is wrong; it is much more a question of who is useful, who is stimulating, who has helped things forward.
>
> (Bondi 1972: 225)

If we wanted to say that an essay, assignment, research report, dissertation or thesis contained evidence as absolute fact, or absolute truth, we would need to be sure that any person anywhere in the world, in any culture, at any time, would reason and come to the same conclusion. That is unlikely to happen, even if there are proofs which *appear* to establish such 'facts' conclusively. The importance of context and value is paramount and emphasized by Rudduck when she writes:

> To call something 'evidence' is not to imply that it carries authority, but merely that it is relevant to the matter under discussion. The witness who is lying or whose memory is playing tricks is giving evidence. . . . A key question for any piece of evidence is: Evidence of what? It may be evidence of a fact or event, but it may also be evidence of a class of events, a kind of situation. A statement may provide evidence of the existence of a point of view or climate of opinion. . . . it may need to be seen in the perspective of the disciplines of knowledge: it may be evidence of the kind of approach to the problem under discussion which is made by an historian, a geographer, a psychologist, a sociologist or a philosopher. And this location in a discipline is in part indicative of the criteria by which a piece of evidence should be judged.
>
> (Rudduck 1983: 18)

So far, I have maintained that evidence is located within a particular discipline and there must be suitable connections within our experience to understand it. The same conclusions about the same evidence may not hold good if the context or subject discipline is a different one. Besides this, there are always aspects of evidence which can be called into question, however good we think the evidence might be. The significance of this for your study is that you are likely to find the issues of 'evidence' and 'contexts' a rich source of controversy. Each subject discipline continually develops the paradigms it adopts, and you consequently need to know where your own work fits the general scheme. Otherwise you are in danger of taking the credibility of evidence for granted.

## COMMON CONFUSIONS ABOUT EVIDENCE

Naturally enough, if you refer to evidence, you must be sure that you do not mean something else, such as 'sources' or 'data'. This is a common confusion for many students and one which is worth clearing up. In some cases, these sources can be collected data, but may include anything from an historical document to a photograph, tape recording or a sheet of calculations. It is surprising how many students do not understand that literary, historical, scientific or sociological sources (or data gathered during a research project) *are not in themselves evidence to support arguments.* Sources and data in both science and the humanities may simply be waiting to be analysed and used to provide evidence. You would have to go a stage further than the source or data itself to find evidence. Sources must be questioned, sifted and analysed before they yield evidence. This may seem obvious, but many students present data as if the status of it were already established.

A practical example from historical research is helpful here. An Edwardian photograph, or a government record, is a source from which evidence can be quarried. It is similar to 'raw data'. As Portal explains:

> Sources are all that remain of the past. There is nothing else. By themselves they constitute a rag-bag of history – the historian's raw material. By themselves they tell nothing beyond the fact of their own existence and their own survival. It is only when a source is appropriately interrogated that it will yield evidence . . . it would be quite reasonable to ask students to compare various types of historical sources and reach conclusions based on this comparison. . . . This evidence can be complete in itself, or it can become a springboard for further investigation. Using a source for evidence means in some way going beyond the information contained in it, and taking into account its logical connection with other events.
>
> (Portal 1990: 8)

'Sources' and 'evidence' are terms which need to be kept apart in their meaning. The student who quotes from a primary source is saying 'This is where the evidence can be found', not 'This source *is* the evidence'. This is why sources such as references in a dissertation or thesis need to be discussed rather than pasted into the text without any analysis or criticism. The source of the evidence must be evaluated before validity and status can be established. For references to evidence from the literature of the discipline, you would be asking 'Is this reference significant?', 'Is it from a seminal work in the field?' or 'Is it from a well-validated piece of research?' 'Is the person or institution cited reputable?' If evidence has been interpreted from data, you would be asking questions such as 'How rigorous was the collection of this data?' and 'How sound is the methodology used to interpret the data to find the evidence?'

In pursuit of quality, two useful questions can separate sources and evidence:

- What is the status of the source from which evidence is extracted?
- What is the status of the evidence itself?

If your written work included research data, you would need to establish that it was gathered from legitimate sources and by legitimate means. Furthermore, you might need to provide a rationale for your decision to use a particular source of data. For example, if you believed that mechanical engineers were the best source of data about vehicle safety standards, you would need to say why. If you believed that teachers were the best source of data for researching classroom practice, you would also need to say why. Otherwise you would be working from a set of assumptions which were never questioned. This is why many disciplines have established formal procedures and criteria for evaluating the sources of data (and the evidence which is interpreted from that data).

## RELIABILITY AND VALIDITY

It follows that lecturers will want to find out how thoroughly you have checked your work to see if it withstands close scrutiny. 'Reliability' tends to be a word usually associated with measurement, but it can also include the extent to which you question the thoroughness with which data has been collected and verified. Reliable evidence is evidence which can be trusted. In some cases, it will be possible to obtain the same data again by repeatedly checking measurements or verifying what people say. The source of the evidence is not prone to variation. Reliability is also associated with the trustworthiness of secondary sources, such as books and research papers. It is a less prominent concern in subjects that involve literary criticism, because interpretation is accepted to be based on whatever theoretical argument the critic proposes. Reliability features prominently in research methodologies where findings need to be verified according to established procedures.

The term 'validity' is used here to mean *checking for anything which might render findings or arguments insecure and therefore invalid.* The main point to remember is that 'validity' is associated with the legality of an argument or permissible use of evidence. An analogy would be that a bicycle could be sufficiently reliable to be on the road, but we might question its valid use on a major motorway. To provide another example: it is possible to make *reliable* measurements of the size of people's feet, but difficult to claim that this is a *valid* measure of intelligence.

The relationship between validity and quality in your written work is substantial. A piece of work which you have done is invalid if it contains contradictory arguments, an unsubstantiated rationale, unreliable data, undeclared biases, prejudices and irrelevancies. Validity in research tends to be especially important because it is so difficult to be sure that research delivers what it says it does. You cannot, for instance, simply assume that data was collected in a valid, 'legal' or 'permissible' way. You may have been so selective that you ignored other evidence which might have been important had you taken the trouble to verify your findings. You might, for example, make the mistake of presenting evidence from research done in 1946 alongside evidence from research done in 1990, while ignoring the credibility gap of forty-four years which you needed to explain.

When you are able to present critical and well-founded arguments, your work can be very impressive indeed:

The key criterion for judging the quality of a dissertation is that students should demonstrate a capacity to critique the theoretical underpinnings of their work.

(Lecturer in Education)

I don't want regurgitated somebody else, I want your judgement, your critique. 'What's the quality of the evidence?' . . . At MA level the distinction for me [of what makes degree work of quality] includes adopting and being able to adopt a critical stance to that which you're reading.

(Professor of Social Work)

If they're critical students, they treat everything they read as if it might be like contaminated food. You don't want to swallow the contents whole and suffer from food-poisoning later on. Make sure you know where the food was bought. Read the 'sell-by' date and the health warnings first.

(Lecturer in Education)

Validity is like a secret weapon of assessment when it comes to determining quality in student study. Within each discipline, what is or is not deemed valid is often understood tacitly through experience of 'living in' the discipline. This is especially true where the validity of references to books, papers and other secondary sources is concerned. Here, you need to make use of the experience of lecturers who know the field very well. They are most likely aware of possible weaknesses associated with various writers and researchers. More formally, there are examples of established research procedures for trying to establish validity. Cohen and Manion (1989), for example, particularly mention validity in experiments, interviews, observation-based research and postal questionnaires.

In some research methods, validating evidence is almost like undertaking a secondary research procedure. Where specific procedures exist (such as triangulation in action-research), validity becomes an issue worthy of discussion in its own right. In academic writing and research, we depend on established procedures to ensure that work has integrity and we put our trust in the knowledge and expertise in which we believe. The problem with procedures for checking evidence is that there is a never-ending argument to be entertained about how to check the validity of the validating procedures themselves. To borrow from Altrichter (1986: 134), there is no way to know in advance whether or not methods for checking validity can be guaranteed in any way. Quoting from House:

> Validation is *a process of responsible argumentation* by which a researcher *checks a research process for invalidities* (i.e. incompatible assumptions concerning the embedded relationships between theory, data and reality) and *tries to reduce them.* Several procedures which suggest different ways of checking are available. However, none of them can conclusively demonstrate the validity of research results. It follows that 'no evaluation approach, no method, will guarantee validity in advance'.
>
> (House 1980: 256)

The problem comes full circle. You are working from a particular 'world view' or paradigm which includes the means by which you validate your study. In turn, your validation affirms the status of your 'world view'. The means within the paradigm are there partly to validate the paradigm itself.

I have suggested that you need to be cautious about presenting evidence. You also need to find out how important validity is within your discipline because of the many interpretations of what it means. It has entirely different connotations and importance for scientists than it does for those concerned with the arts. For literary critics, validity may not be a very important issue. In research into areas such as the arts, the canons of scientific test reliability and sampling simply do not apply. Whether evidence proves something true or false is not the purpose of the research. Eisner comments:

> Validity in the arts is the product of the persuasiveness of a personal vision; its utility is determined by the extent to which it informs. There is no test of statistical significance, no measure of construct validity in artistically rendered research ... The proof of the pudding is the way in which it shapes our conceptions of the world or some aspect of it ... Artistic approaches to research are less concerned with the discovery of truth than with the creation of meaning. What art seeks is not the discovery of the laws of nature, but rather the creation of images that people will find meaningful and from which their fallible and tentative views of the world can be altered, rejected or made more secure.
>
> (Eisner 1985: 191)

What is more interesting is the consequence of taking up particular positions concerning whether research methods and procedures are valid. If, for example, we rejected the view that qualitative, artistic approaches to research are valid ways to research, there would not be much use in taking the next step and examining the meanings they generated. If we thought that measurement and statistics had no place in research that concerned people, we would find it difficult to accept outcomes of these as valid. On the other hand, if we accepted that evidence could take many different and valid forms, meaning could be established according to the context in which it was made.

Questions which you might ask about evidence are:

- What are its sources?
- Are those sources legitimate?
- Are those sources reliable?
- How selective is the data?
- Is the evidence relevant?
- Who says what about the data or sources used?
- How and why do they say it?

- What is the status of the evidence? (How credible/important/relevant?)
- How has it been processed (e.g. statistics)?
- How is the evidence validated? (What bias might there be?)
- How is evidence located in this discipline?

You have several options when you are writing a research-based essay or dissertation. The following (or a combination of some of them) may prove useful. You can:

- ignore validity because it is not a problem
- declare the limitations of reliability
- use established validation procedures
- discuss problems of reliability and validity
- declare assumptions on which your work rests
- include and criticize the rationale for your procedures
- evaluate the paradigm from which you are working

**DOUBT AND RIGOUR**

Taking an extreme position, you could make doubt a healthy principle of your study. You could doubt your secondary references, their context, research methods, your analysis of data, validation procedures and all manner of personal beliefs. There is some virtue in taking the position of someone trying to convince a sceptical reader of your written work. In practice, doubt acts best as a healthy ingredient of rigour, rather than the destructive force it might become if we do not keep a sense of proportion. We certainly cannot question everything *at the same time*. The only way we can offer a reason for questioning something is by appeal to something else that is not, in itself, being questioned.

A frequently quoted story encapsulates the wisdom of doubt and uncertainty. This is the claim that 'all swans are white'. For thousands of years, the population of Europe believed that all swans were white because all the evidence pointed to that conclusion. It took a trip to Australia to discover that swans can also be black (the moral of the story being 'Never rule out the possibility that you might be wrong'). But like many discoveries, it is difficult to see what this has done for the world apart from becoming a classic example of evidence forcing a shift in the accepted paradigm. Could it be that the white swans example has become most useful as the researcher's cautionary tale?

Any theory, any assertion, always has to have an element of doubt. . . . For those of us whose lifestyle is based on thinking, thorough thinking, rigorous thinking, the search for truth is a tentative process. It's contrary to human nature in a way, in that most of us lust for certainty, which is why fundamentalists exist . . . it's very comfortable to live in a world of certainty. It's an unreal world, though. Life is uncertain, everything about truth is uncertain, all theories don't prove anything, they can only be used to disprove things, and so it goes on.

(PhD student)

No examiner is looking for unequivocal certainties in your work and may be reassured if you are cautious enough in what you claim. You establish the context in which evidence is presented to reduce the possibility of misinterpretation. To be rigorous you would also take account of a wide variety of views, doubts and uncertainties:

A student [who was researching] might use constructs for guiding the methodology and analysing data. But these might embody all sorts of assumptions . . . so what you want the student to do is to be aware that there could be a debate about the adequacy of these constructs in explaining and interpreting data. You'd want them to make that clear to the reader so you knew they had taken these things into account.

(Professor of Education)

Lack of rigour would comprise a partial presentation of the issues, the reality. . . . It would be too narrow a covering of the field, only looking at a part of the available material. It's incomplete.

(Professor of Social Work)

A lack of rigour would be if, without using any accredited approach for analysing the literature, I thought 'Oh, I'll just read it through and pick out a few key words and I'll write a thousand words on those' . . . that would not be rigorous. It's too uncertain, too *laissez-faire*, too self-centred, too arrogant . . . all words which I'd apply to a lack of rigour.

(PhD student)

It [lack of rigour] means for me that the work hasn't mobilized enough information, whether it be references or primary data, or whatever might convince me from my perspective. It might have convinced somebody who's in another discipline, but rigour is defined by the institutional context in which you're working.

(Lecturer in Economics)

At the risk of sounding very boring, I'd say that it [rigour] really is a question of how well you are able to locate what you are doing in the discipline. It's a question of your proficiency in using the techniques of your subject.

(Lecturer in Development Studies)

I would look for evidence that they [the students] had sought out evidence which challenged their own assumptions . . . evidence of some comparison of perspectives leading them to make the attempt to explain and argue a case.

(Professor of Education)

What I say to research students is that, if you know there's a limitation, tell your External Examiner. Don't wait to be told it's a limitation. I mean, the examiner might say, 'I don't think you can ignore that. I think that was a serious error of judgement to ignore that because it is too profound a mistake.'

(Professor of Education)

## MEANING-MAKING, OTHERS AND SELF

When you provide evidence to support your claims, you are declaring the grounds on which meaning has been made. Of course, it is all very well to suggest that this might be a logical process. An oversimple view to take is that you:

1  establish the context in which you intend to be understood
2  define your terms within that context
3  interpret and substantiate your views with evidence
4  tell us how significant the findings are

Yet study, research and writing are not necessarily isolated logical activities, having no relationship with the way people live their lives. Logical argument is necessary, but you should not be misled into thinking that the story ends there. Apart from developing the ability to comprehend in critical, logical and well-argued ways, you have another important task. Your concern is to relate what evidence you find to a much wider context of utility, ethics and human understanding.

This is an aspect of meaning-making which concerns you in relation to others. If this were not so, studying would be limited to developing your intellect while ignoring the imaginative use to which that intellect might be put. The very reason for studying is that it reveals a vision of the world you have not previously encountered. Polanyi and Prosch (1975: 104) lend support to this when they describe how the utility of a movement in art, such as French Impressionism, 'lies in the imaginative powers unleashed by the new vision'. They compare this with the criteria by which we might judge science, but they do not fall into the trap of thinking science is ultimately about logical proof: 'The world view projected by science [is properly judged] . . . by the attraction of the imaginative powers set free by this vision of the world. The extension of scientific thinking into the formation of a world view is *a work of the imagination*, not of the formally critical intellect.' You are therefore making meaning from your study for yourself as well as communicating to an examiner or your lecturers. The formally critical intellect is an important tool for establishing a logical argument based on sound evidence; here we have an echo of the point I was making earlier. Logic is of limited use if it does not become stimulating or useful for the matter in hand. An argument can be logical without reflecting the experience to which it purports to relate. For example, intuitively, most of us would accept the assertion that problems exist and discoveries can be made by solving them. However, the philosopher Plato took a more depressing view:

> To search for the solution of a problem is an absurdity; for either you know what you are looking for, and then there is no problem; or you do not know what you are looking for, and then you cannot expect to find anything.
>
> (quoted in Polanyi 1967: 22)

This is one of those delightful arguments which begs a human context to make better sense of it. As we know from experience, it is perfectly possible for a student to write about problems and solutions without this seeming absurd. People take for granted that the problem–solution mode of living is validated by their experience. Nevertheless, as Polanyi goes on to say: 'For two thousand years and more, humanity has progressed through the efforts of people solving difficult problems, while all the time it could [logically] be shown that to do this was either meaningless or impossible.'

Pursuing the point further, human beings engage in a variety of activities which may not involve much logical reasoning, but nevertheless have great significance for them. Falling in love, listening to music, smelling the roses and signing their name are just some. When we learn something we cannot confine knowledge to information, procedures or logic alone. An early view of the way we learn saw the mind as a blank sheet of paper or as uninformed clay, ready to receive impressions. Yet we learn, not just in one way, bit by bit, but in a variety of ways for a variety of reasons. Norman (1978) provides an interesting explanation. Apart from the process of adding, bit by bit, to what we already understand, we fine-tune and restructure what we have already learned. For example, a child might understand bit by bit what metal items are attracted by a magnet. Any new item which proves to be magnetic is simply added to the list of 'things that are magnetic'. Similar claims could be made for the way in which children add words to a growing vocabulary or a gardener adds names of plants to a list of perennials. *Fine-tuning*, however, is where we remove redundant stages in understanding something, such as in discarding sections of an instruction manual once we develop some basic understanding of how to operate without it. *Restructuring* is where our understanding undergoes radical change. New evidence or experience causes us to restructure the concept, paradigm or 'world view' we previously entertained.

Here is where meaning-making is particularly important yet at its most difficult to explain. Where Norman's other two aspects of learning involve memory and discarding information, restructuring requires us to appraise previous understanding and develop or change it. There are always interlocking patterns of thoughts, beliefs and biases which determine our conceptions. Evidence can come into conflict with belief and reverberate against all we have previously encountered. Studying is therefore not just a matter of being introduced to information and the working conventions of a subject discipline. The point is captured by Elliott when he says:

> Education is not simply a matter of developing human powers of understanding by inducting students into 'structures of

knowledge'. It is about developing these powers in relation to the things which matter in life. Chess is a sophisticated and complex activity which provides opportunities for people to develop a range of complex skills and abilities. But it is nevertheless a game. The problems of chess have little significance as problems of living. It is in relation to the latter that the powers of human understanding must be developed if such a process is to count as an educational one.

(Elliott 1991: 147)

In your study you will no doubt experience the convention and tedium of repeatedly checking findings and evidence. Yet, if study is not to be a wholly dull affair, its reward must lie elsewhere, in inspiration, as well as within 'structures of knowledge'. Few lecturers are prepared to explain 'the study system' because *there is no system*. There are many vital and exciting ways to study. Although you may study so that you gain an award, the process of studying anything does far more than measure your achievement in order to award a qualification. The attraction of study is to be left with the possibility that the world is a much larger and more inspiring place than you knew before you began.

## CHECK LIST SUMMARY

- Sound uses of evidence rely on drawing analogies with known cases of the same pattern.
- Sound uses of evidence are not a proof that the conclusion follows logically from the evidence: they show that the conclusion is probable on the evidence.
- Before anything can be challenged, we first have to understand how it is located within a discipline and how that discipline argues its principles and values.
- It matters a great deal that you understand what is meant by *good evidence* within your own discipline.
- You cannot assume a universal understanding of the terms 'fact' or 'factual evidence'.
- The status of evidence is determined by its value, significance and relevance to your research or writing.
- Evidence should not be confused with sources/data.
- In pursuit of quality, two useful questions are these:

  1 What is the status and reliability of the source from which evidence is quarried?
  2 What is the status of the evidence itself?

- Evidence can come into conflict with belief and reverberate against all we have previously encountered.
- Examiners, lecturers and other readers bring their own meanings to the content of something you write or discuss with them.
- To examine criteria at the beginning of your study and attempt to fulfil them is missing the point.

## ACTION PLAN

- Find out what your lecturers perceive as 'good evidence'.
- Find out what criteria exist for assessing your work.
- Ask for criteria to be explained if you do not understand.
- Be aware that the extent to which study can stimulate and reveal a greater vision of the world may matter more than its limitations.

# References

Altrichter, H. (1986) 'Visiting two worlds: an excursion into the methodological jungle including an optional evening's entertainment at the Rigour Club', *Cambridge Journal of Education* 16 (2).

Bell, C. and Roberts, H. (eds) (1984) *Social Researching, Politics, Problems, Practice*, London: Routledge & Kegan Paul.

Best, D. (1985) *Feeling and Reason in the Arts*, London: Allen & Unwin.

Blanchard, J. and Mikkelson, V. (1987) 'Underlining performance outcomes in expository test', *Journal of Educational Research* 80 (4): 197–201.

Bondi, H. (1972) 'The achievements of Karl Popper', *The Listener*, 88 (2265): 225–9, quoted in D. Best (1985) *Feeling and Reason in the Arts*, London: Allen & Unwin, p. 26.

Bowles, G. and Duelli Klein, R. (eds) (1983) *Theories of Women's Studies*, London: Routledge & Kegan Paul.

Boyd, H.W. and Westfall, R. (1979) 'Interviewer bias once more revisited', in J. Bynner and K.M. Stribley (1979) *Social Research*, NY: Longman, pp. 171–8.

Buzan, A. (1974) *Use Your Head*, London: BBC Publications.

Bynner, J. and Stribley, K.M. (1979) *Social Research: Principles and Procedures*, New York: Longman.

Carr, W. and Kemmis, S. (1986) *Becoming Critical: Education, Knowledge and Action Research*, London: The Falmer Press.

Cohen, L. and Manion, L. (1989) *Research Methods in Education*, 3rd edn, London: Routledge.

Collee, J. (1990) 'A doctor writes', *The Observer*, 10 November.

Eisner, E. (1985) *The Art of Educational Evaluation: a Personal View*, London: The Falmer Press.

Elliott, J. (1991) *Action Research for Educational Change*, London: Open University Press.

Entwistle, N. and Wilson, J. (1977) *Degrees of Excellence: The Academic Achievement Game*, London: Hodder & Stoughton.

Flesch, R.F. (1951) *How to Test Readability*, New York: Harper & Brothers.

Flew, A. (1975) *Thinking about Thinking*, London: Fontana Press.

—— (1979) *A Dictionary of Philosophy*, London: Pan Books.

Fromm, E. (1979) *To Have or To Be?*, 2nd edn, London: Sphere Books.
Garrett, H.E. (1947) *Statistics in Psychology and Education*, New York: Longmans, Green.
Gehlbach, R. (1990) 'Art education: issues in curriculum and research', *Educational Researcher* 19 (7): 19–25.
Gibaldi, J. and Achtert, W.S. (1977) *The MLA Handbook for Writers of Research Papers, Theses and Dissertations*, New York: Modern Language Association.
Gibbs, G. (1977) 'Can students be taught how to study?', *Higher Education Bulletin* 5 (2): 107–18.
Hakim, C. (1987) *Research Design: Strategies and Choices in the Design of Social Research*, London: Allen & Unwin.
Hammersley, M. and Atkinson, P. (1983) *Ethnography: Principles in Practice*, London: Open University Press.
Handy, C. and Aitken, R. (1986) *Understanding Schools as Organizations*, London: Penguin.
Hofstadter, D. (1985) *Metamagical Themas*, Harmondsworth: Penguin.
Hollis, M. (1985) *Invitation to Philosophy*, Oxford: Basil Blackwell.
Hounsell, D. (1984) 'Learning and essay writing', in F. Marton *et al.* (1984) *The Experience of Learning*, Edinburgh: Scottish Academic Press, pp. 103–23.
House, E.R. (1980) *Evaluating with Validity*, Beverly Hills: Sage.
Idstein, P. and Jenkins, J.R. (1972) 'Underlining versus repetitive reading', *Journal of Educational Research* 65 (7): 321–3.
Kuhn, T.S. (1970) *The Structure of Scientific Revolutions*, Chicago: University of Chicago Press.
Lowenthal, D. and Wason, P.C. (1977) 'Academics and their writing', in E.M. Phillips and D.S. Pugh (1987) *How to get a PhD*, London: Open University Press.
McBride, R. (ed.) (1989) *The In-Service Training of Teachers*, London: The Falmer Press.
Mackay, A.L. (1977) *The Harvest of a Quiet Eye*, London: Institute of Physics.
McNeill, P. (1990) *Research Methods*, 2nd edn, London: Routledge.
Maddox, H. (1988) *How to Study*, 2nd edn, London: Pan Books.
Maney, A.S. and Smallwood, R.L. (eds) (1971) *MHRA Style Book: Notes for Authors and Editors*, London: Modern Humanities Research Association.
Marshall, L.A. and Rowland, F. (1983) *A Guide to Learning Independently*, London: Open University Press.
Marton, F., Hounsell, D. and Entwistle, N. (1984) *The Experience of Learning*, Edinburgh: Scottish Academic Press.
Mead, M. (1935) *Sex and Temperament in Three Primitive Societies*, New York: William Morrow.
Messick, S. (1988) 'Validity', in R.L. Linn (ed.) *Educational Measurement*, 3rd edn, New York: Macmillan, pp. 13–103.
Norman, D.A. (1978) 'Notes towards a complex theory of learning', in A.M. Lesgold, J.W. Pellegrino, D.F. Sipke and R. Glaser (eds) *Cognitive Psychology and Instruction*, New York: Plenum.

—— (1982) *Learning and Memory*, Oxford: Freeman.
Pateman, T. (1987) *What is Philosophy?*, London: Edward Arnold.
Phillips, E. M. and Pugh, D.S. (1987) *How to get a PhD*, London: Open University Press.
Polanyi, M. (1967) *The Tactit Dimension*, London: Routledge & Kegan Paul.
Polanyi, M. and Prosch, H. (1975) *Meaning*, London: University of Chicago Press.
Portal, C. (ed.) (1990) *Sources in History; From Definition to Assessment*, 2nd edn, London: Longman Group in association with the Southern Region Examining Board.
Rowntree, D. (1988) *Learn How to Study*, 3rd edn, London: Macdonald & Company.
Rudduck, J. (1978) *Learning through Small Group Discussion: a Study of Seminar Work in Higher Education*, Guildford: Society for Research into Higher Education.
—— (1983) *The Humanities Curriculum Project: An Introduction*, revised edn, Norwich: School of Education, University of East Anglia for the Schools Council.
Russell, P. (1979) *The Brain Book*, London: Routledge & Kegan Paul.
Säljö, R. (1984) 'Learning from reading', in Marton *et al.* (1984) *The Experience of Learning*, Edinburgh: Scottish Academic Press, pp. 71–89.
Satow, A. and Evans, M. (1983) *Working with Groups*, London: Tacade and The Health Education Council.
Sheppard, R. (1990) 'From Narragoinia to Elysium: some preliminary reflections on the fictional image of the academic', in D. Bevan (ed.), *University Fiction*, Rodopi Perspectives on Modern Literature, vol. 5, Amsterdam/Atlanta, GA: Editions Rodopi, pp. 11–48.
Smith, F. (1971) *Understanding Reading*, London: Holt, Rinehart & Winston.
Stanley, L. and Wise, S. (1983) 'Back into the personal or: our attempt to construct feminist research', in G. Bowles and R. Duclli Klein (1983) *Theories of Women's Studies*, London: Routledge & Kegan Paul, pp. 192–209.
Strunk, W. Jr and White, E.B. (1972) *The Elements of Style*, New York: Macmillan.
Thouless, R.H. and Thouless, C.R. [1930] (1990) *Straight and Crooked Thinking*, London: Hodder & Stoughton.
Wainer, H. and Braun, H. (1988) *Test Validity*, Hillsdale, NJ: Lawrence Erlbaum.
Wason, P.C. (1974) 'Notes on the supervision of PhDs', *Bulletin of the British Psychological Society* 27: 25–9.
Winter, R. (1989) *Learning from Experience*, London: The Falmer Press.

# Index